Unshakable Freedom:

Choose this book

Chuck Chakrapani reveals for modern eyes what the ancient Stoics knew: True freedom comes from choosing wisely. Here's an aligned piece of advice – choose this book.

Robert Cialdini PhD,
Author *Influence* and *Pre-suasion*

Fast, interesting, and it works

Chuck Chakrapani brings Stoic philosophy to the world of today, the world in which we live, love, compete, win, lose, but never escape. Our world. The early Stoics and those who succeeded them have much to teach, but it takes a thoughtful writer to give us this wisdom in the way WE NEED TO LEARN. Chuck is one of those writers. Read this book ...it's fast, interesting, but most of all it WORKS.

Dr. Howard Moskowitz,
Chief Science Officer, Mind Genomics Advisors

A timely and readable reminder

We live in a time when happiness and autonomy are commonly equated with higher levels of and options for consumption. This little book is a timely and readable reminder that the path to enjoyment and independence lies elsewhere.

Thomas Dunk PhD,
Dean, Faculty of Social Sciences, Brock University

[This book] can change your life for good

Unshakable Freedom *is a wonderful guide to those who want real freedom and peace in a complex and challenging world. It also vividly portrays many of the leaders and prominent people who have found success by following these principles. It really can change your life for good.*

Ashref Hashim,
President, The Blackstone Group

For greater productivity, prosperity and inner peace

In Unshakable Freedom, *Chuck identifies that the only thing stopping us from being happy is ourselves. The Stoic tenants outlined, if followed, will lead to greater productivity, prosperity, and inner peace for the reader. Thanks to Chuck for the inspiration!*

Dr. Kara Mitchelmore,
CEO, Marketing Research & Intelligence Association

Immediately practical

Chuck Chakrapani has written this wonderful book of timeless, immensely practical messages to help us generate powerful real-world impact and remind us how to stay free and appreciative. Unshakable Freedom *provides an immediately practical lesson to gain freedom and personal power.*

Sabine Steinbrecher,
CEO, The Learning Library

Designed to improve quality of life

Unshakable Freedom *is about finding peace of mind. Stoic philosophy is a tool to address daily travails - big and small. The author has proposed techniques designed to lead to freedom, happiness, and a better quality of life. I recommend that you go through the book slowly, absorb, and practice.*

Naresh Malhotra
CEO Global, Novatrek

A Fortunate Storm
A Companion Volume to *Unshakable Freedom*

Unshakable Freedom is based on Stoic teachings.

But how did Stoicism come about?

Three unconnected events – a shipwreck in Piraeus, a play in Thebes, and the banishment of a rebel in Turkey – connected three unrelated individuals to give birth to a philosophy. It was to endure two thousand years and offer hope and comfort to hundreds of thousands of people along the way.

The Fortunate Storm is the improbable story of how Stoicism came about. You can get a FREE COPY of the e-version of this book at the link below:

http://www.TheStoicGym.com/fortunatestormfree

Unshakable Freedom

ANCIENT STOIC SECRETS
APPLIED TO MODERN LIFE

Chuck Chakrapani, PhD

The Stoic Gym Publications

The Stoic Gym
A Standard Research Systems Imprint

For bulk ordering and rights permissions requests, please visit http://thestoicgym.com.
First Edition.
ISBNs
Print: 978-0-920219-18-8
ePub: 978-0-920219-19-5
Mobi: 978-0-920219-20-1
PDF: 978-0-920219-21-8

25 24 23 22 21 20 19 18 17 16   1 2 3 4 5 6 7 8 9

Contents

Don't you know that freedom is a glorious thing of great worth?

EPICTETUS

The Festival of Life

I have this purpose: to complete you, to free you from restraint,
compulsion, hindrance, to make you free, prosperous, and
happy ... And you are here to practice these things.

Epictetus[1]

F or most of us, freedom is an ideal not really achieved in
our everyday life. We try to keep our jobs, to live within
a limited income, not to offend others, and to avoid un-
necessary arguments. We worry about life passing us
by, about our jobs, our children, and our parents. We don't even
realize how unfree we are while we go on with life, walking on
eggshells.

Anxiety about the future, fear of illness and old age, and constant replaying of the past keep us trapped. When we are free to
choose, the choice seems to be between two unattractive alter-
natives. Do we want to continue in our miserable job or face

unemployment? Do we want to argue with our spouse or invite a boring couple for dinner?

As Thoreau observed, "The mass of men lead lives of quiet desperation."[2] Where's the freedom in that?

We are robbed of our liberty not only by everyday life problems, but also by terrorists, the government, the economy, society, our jobs, and a hundred other obligations. Is freedom still possible?

Yes, say the Stoics. Stoicism was founded around 2,300 years ago. Following that, Stoicism flourished in Greece and Rome for about five centuries. There are many misconceptions about Stoicism, such as Stoics are humorless, they internally suffer and don't show it, they are emotionless, etc. Yet the Stoics discovered a way of life based on personal freedom, which was joyful and serene no matter what else was going on around them.

If you would like to be free from all things that enslave you, Stoics say they can show you how. No one can take away your freedom without your permission. Not terrorists, nor the government, the economy, society, your job, your obligations, the past, your family, or your spouse.

If we clearly understand what is under our control and what is not, we can achieve freedom simply by exercising our control. We don't need to wait for anyone to do anything. We don't have to make a million dollars or ten; to run away from where we are. We don't need anyone's permission, and we don't need to change anyone. We have all we need to achieve freedom. It is as simple as that.

Stoics didn't mince their words. They didn't hedge their bets. Just listen to Epictetus: "I have this purpose: to complete you, to free you from restraint, compulsion, hindrance, to make you free, prosperous, and happy... And you are here to practice these things."[3]

That's a big promise. Not an empty one, either. People have practiced Stoicism for over two thousand years and found that it worked for them. Since I picked up a copy of the Stoic Emperor, Marcus Aurelius', book *Meditations* when I was in my teens, Stoicism has provided me comfort throughout my life. It offered me solace when I was troubled, encouraged me when things looked bleak, and steadied me when I wobbled, even though I have been an inconsistent and imperfect practitioner of the philosophy.

Stoicism is not an exclusive philosophy open only to a few. It is open to anyone. So why is the book's subtitle "Ancient Stoic Secrets"? The Stoic techniques are "secrets" only because so little of Stoicism is known to the general public, in spite of its resurging popularity.

This book is about what I learned from Stoicism about freedom. Since Stoicism was established, the meaning of words has changed. I have chosen to interpret Stoic teachings in terms of what they would likely mean now, while trying to be true to their spirit.[4]

More than anything else, I want to share with you that Stoicism is as practical in today's digital world as it was two thousand years ago. I have included many contemporary examples of people living the Stoic way. They are active members of society, not reclusive philosophers. I have even included some examples of stoic actions of people who are not formal practitioners of Stoic philosophy.

Becoming comfortable with a few profound ideas is much more important, it seems to me, than pursuing tons of trivial ones. I have expressed the same ideas in different words in different places, used deliberate repetition, and illustrated them with examples, so the basic ideas are well-absorbed.

I hope this book captures the basic spirit of Stoic freedom and what it means to be free and to participate in the festival of life.

PART I

CHOOSE FREEDOM

Freedom is a choice. Choose it.

CHAPTER 1

Freedom is a choice

If you choose, you are free; if you choose, you need to blame no one and accuse no one.

Epictetus[5]

Someone informed Agrippinus[6] that his trial was going on in the Senate. Agrippinus replied, "I hope it turns out in my favor. But it is eleven in the morning. Time for me to work out and take a bath. Let me be off." After Agrippinus had his exercise, a friend walked in.

"You have been condemned."

"To death or exile?"

"Exile."

"What about my property?"

"It is not taken from you."

"Then let's go to my villa in Aricia and have lunch there."

This is the essence of freedom. You are on trial. Yes, but that is no reason not to enjoy your workout and your bath now. You have been banished. Yes, but that is no reason not to go else-where and have a nice lunch. You live your life such that free-dom comes from things that are under your control.

We can achieve freedom by controlling what we can and leaving the rest to others. Whether the Senate tries you or not is beyond your control. But whether you want to be upset about it or enjoy your workout and a bath now *is* under your control. Whether you are exiled or not is not under your control. But whether you want to feel miserable about it or whether you want to enjoy your lunch elsewhere *is* under your control.

Agrippinus chose to exercise, take a bath, and enjoy his lunch elsewhere, because he chose what was under his control. Most of us do the exact opposite. We choose to be upset by the trial; feel miserable that we are banished; and refuse to enjoy the workout, the bath, and the lunch. We are defeated by the choices we make, not by what happens to us. We try to control what is beyond our control and ignore what is under our control. This is no way to be free.

Try to enjoy the great festival of life now. Don't lament that it wasn't there all the time. Or that won't be there tomorrow. Enjoy the festival as long as it lasts. If it ends, let it go.

This is central to freedom: freedom flows from controlling what is under our control; frustration flows from trying to con-trol what is not under our control. Choose not to be crushed or depressed by whatever happens. "If you choose, you are free. If you choose, you need to blame no one, to accuse no one"[7]. We all possess this freedom within us.

Agrippinus was a Stoic philosopher who lived two thousand years ago. Would this kind of thinking work in our world today where we have wars, we have terrorists, we have no job security, and the future is more unpredictable than ever? Would it work even if we don't have deep philosophic training? Would it work if you are a woman brutally raped? Let's see.

She went to war

Rhonda Cornum,[8] a flight surgeon during the first Gulf War, was on a mission to rescue a fighter pilot who had been shot down. Soon her helicopter was shot down as well. She survived but with a torn ligament in her knee and two broken arms. She was taken prisoner by Iraqi soldiers, the first female prisoner of war anywhere in the world since WWII.

While being transported in a truck, one of the Iraqi soldiers sexually molested her. "Weighing just 110 pounds on a 5-foot-6 frame, with both of her arms broken and a bullet in her back, she couldn't fight. If she bit her assailant, she worried he'd hit her and break even more bones."[9]

She was imprisoned for eight days after that. During this time she was subjected to a mock execution. Thus she endured physical harm, molestation when she was physically helpless, incarceration, and mental torture, all at about the same time.

One would suppose that the whole thing would have been terribly traumatic for her, not only when it happened but for years to come, even permanently. But that was not her reaction. Instead, she said that what she learned was, "that the experience doesn't have to be devastating [and] that it depends on you." She further said, "You're supposed to look at being sexually molested as a fate worse than death. Having faced both, I can tell you it's not. Getting molested was not the biggest deal of my life." How did she approach every problem she encountered? "I would fix what I could fix, and I wouldn't complain about what I couldn't."

In an interview with the *New York Times*, she said the sexual assault, "ranks as unpleasant; that's all it ranks... everyone's made such a big deal about this indecent assault, but the only thing that makes it indecent is that it was nonconsensual. I asked myself, 'Is it going to prevent me from getting out of here? Is there a risk of death attached to it? Is it permanently disabling? Is it permanently disfiguring? Lastly, is it excruciating?' If it doesn't fit one of those five categories, then it isn't important." Rhonda Cornum's comment, "that the experience doesn't have to be devastating... it depends on you," is the essence of Stoicism.

Cornum chose not to be miserable. She chose not to be beaten by what most people would consider a highly traumatizing experience. She continued to be productive. She chose freedom over self-pity. Cornum rose to the rank of Brigadier General and became one of only seven women in history to receive the Distinguished Flying Cross. She productively served in the US Army until she was 58 and retired in 2012.

I am not sure if Rhonda Cornum was exposed to Stoicism before these traumatic things happened to her. However, she thought like a Stoic, focusing more on what *was* under her control rather than being crushed by what *was not* under her control.

How is it possible to enjoy your lunch when you have just been exiled? How is it possible to stay calm when you have just been raped? How can we choose differently?

You have the power to choose

"Between stimulus and response, there is space. In that space is our power to choose our response. In our response lies our growth and our freedom." That's Dr. Viktor Frankl, speaking.

He should know.

In 1942, Austrian psychiatrist Viktor Frankl, his wife, and parents were deported to the Nazi Theresienstadt ghetto. His father died there. In 1944, Frankl and his wife were moved to Auschwitz concentration camp and then to several other camps. He was allowed to live because, as a physician, the Nazis considered him useful. During his imprisonment, he witnessed horrors of degradation and death. This continued every day until 1945 when he was liberated by American soldiers.

One day, while still incarcerated, he realized that no matter what happened, he was free. He realized that everything could be taken away from him, even his life. But he was free to think what he pleased, to choose his response. And he did. Even though he was physically unfree, he remained mentally free. Free of sorrow, free of anguish, free of fear. He put it this way: "Everything can be taken away from a man but one thing: the last of the human freedoms – to choose one's attitude in any given circumstances, to choose one's own way."[10]

We can choose to wallow in self-pity and misery, or choose to be free. We will not be able to avoid pain. But we won't be adding sorrow to our pain. We will not be able to avoid disease, old age, or death. But we won't live in fear. We will not be delivered from injustice. But we won't be hurt by it. We can be free no matter what.

Choosing freedom

Twenty years later in 1965, during the Vietnam War, Vice Admiral James Stockdale was the commander of the air group CAG. Hit by anti-aircraft fire; he was ejected and broke a bone in his back. As he hit the ground, he dislocated his knee. He remained a prisoner of war for nearly 8 years in Hoa Lo Prison (nicknamed "Hanoi Hilton"). During this time he was subjected to repeated torture. For the first few years in prison, he could not even stand up because of his broken leg. He was subjected to solitary confinement, in total darkness, for four years. Yet he never gave out any secrets.

What helped him to choose his own freedom – whether he would disclose any secrets or not – were Stoic principles he had learned earlier. Epictetus' words, "lameness is an impediment to the body but not to the will," provided him the strength to endure his fractured leg. His captors could imprison his body but not his mind. While being subjected to torture for more than seven years, he chose to be free and not be coerced into doing things he did not want to do. After his release, he carried on serving in the US navy and retired in 1971 with the rank of Navy Vice Admiral.

He continued to be active and was Ross Perot's running mate in the 1992 US presidential election. James Stockdale explicitly acknowledged the influence of Stoic philosophy in facing whatever life threw at him, including about eight years of torture in a prison.

We cannot control what life hands us: Senate trial, physical harm, violent molestation, concentration camp, or prison. But we don't need to be crushed by any of it. There is nothing in life that can't be handled. If we choose, there is no situation in which we are not free. The road to freedom is also the road to happiness.

Stoics discovered the principles of freedom over 2,000 years ago. Let's see what Stoicism has to teach us about how we can set ourselves free and find freedom and happiness even when the world around us is unfree and unhappy.

CHAPTER 2

What the Stoics Knew That We Don't

Just because you've abandoned your hopes of becoming a great thinker or scientist, don't give up on attaining freedom.

Marcus Aurelius[11]

U nlike philosophers of today, ancient philosophers were mostly concerned about everyday life: how to live the good life in freedom and happiness no matter who you were, where you lived, or what you did, whether you were rich or poor. Philosophers then were self-help gurus, the original lifehackers. Lao Tzu, Confucius, Buddha, Zeno of Citium, Diogenes, Epicurus, Epictetus, and a host of others were concerned about the human condition and how to achieve freedom and happiness.

All Greek philosophers around this time wanted to show how to achieve the good life or "eudemonia". *How* to achieve it is where they differed. Our focus is on Stoicism, which bears more than a passing resemblance to Buddhism.

According to Stoics, one could achieve the good life by being "virtuous." What is being virtuous? It is living according to nature. What is living according to nature? It is living according to reason.

The Stoics argued that, compared to other animals, humans are not the strongest; they are not the fastest or the best swimmers, and they cannot fly. However, they have that unique faculty, reason, not shared by other animals. Thus, "living in agreement with nature," means living in agreement with our special gift – our ability to reason. Therefore, if you lead a life based on reason, you live according to nature. As Marcus Aurelius held, "an act that is according to nature is also an act according to reason."[12] Living according to nature is a "virtuous" life. Freedom, which is an aspect of the good life, is the result of living virtuously.

Stoic "virtue" is somewhat different from what we mean by virtue when we use the word these days. Virtue in Stoicism did not mean following a moral code with probity. For the Stoics, living virtuously meant living rationally. It is a life characterized by *wisdom* (resourcefulness and discretion), *justice* (honesty), *courage*, and *moderation*.

Similarly, the Stoics divided vice into *foolishness, injustice, cowardice, intemperance*, and *the rest*. A person who lives rationally would be wise, just, courageous, and moderate.

Over the centuries, Stoicism has offered comfort and guidance not only to emperors, army generals, and heads of states, but to ordinary people and even to slaves. Stoic freedom is equally available whether you are an emperor or a slave, whether you work from nine to five in a cubicle or are unemployed. It is as available today as it was over 2,000 years ago. It is as relevant to us today as it was to emperors and slaves of ancient Rome and Greece.

In ancient Greece and Rome, competing philosophers tried to get converts to their way of thinking by addressing people in public, not unlike modern-day evangelists. Some philosophers used the public square. Stoics got their name because they used to teach under a *stoa poikile* (painted porch).

The Stoic school was founded by Zeno of Citium in Athens in the early 3ʳᵈ Century BCE. He taught that negative emotions such as anger, fear, depression, worry, and anxiety resulted from errors in thinking. Stoicism is an antidote to all emotional ills and a guide to the good life. Because it is a way of life, it is not what a person says but how that person behaves. To live a good life, one has to understand the rules of the natural order of things. This can be taught to others so they can lead the good life, free from fear, worry, and anxiety.

There have been several Stoic philosophers – Musonius Rufus, Cleanthes, Agrippinus, Cato, Seneca, Epictetus, Aurelius to name a few – since that time. Stoicism was popular even in its early days and had followers in Greece and the Roman Empire. Less than 1% of the original literature survives today, most of it by the later Roman Stoics who lived between the birth of Christ and 150 CE and whose body of work is now widely available. Later Stoics, in particular Seneca, Epictetus, and Aurelius taught that "virtue" (living according to natural order) is sufficient for happiness. A sage is immune to misfortune and outside conditions have no effect on "Stoic calm".

As you will see from the following stories of Seneca, Epictetus, and Aurelius, they were not simply theoretical philosophers. They were men who lived varied and colorful lives, fully immersed in the drama of everyday events. Their lives were very different. They all faced different kinds of hardships and challenges but were unmoved by them, leading lives of freedom, tranquility, and contentment.

Seneca, the royal tutor who lived in luxury

Lucius Annaeus Seneca, (Seneca, the Younger) was born around 4 BCE in Cordoba in Spain and raised in Rome. Seneca became an orator and, while in Rome, he made a powerful speech which aroused the Emperor Caligula's jealousy. He spared Seneca's life only because he believed Seneca would die soon. The reprieve did not last long. Messalina, the wife of the next emperor, Claudius, accused Seneca of committing adultery with the Emperor's niece, Julia Livilla, and had him banished in 41 CE.

Several years later, Seneca returned to Rome and became first a tutor to Nero and later his advisor when Nero became Emperor. Because of his position, he lived well. He had more than 300 million sestertii, making him a multimillionaire by today's standards. He also owned several villas and vineyards around Italy. He was said to have lived in luxury, owning 500 identical citrus-wood tables with ivory legs that he used when he threw lavish dinner parties to entertain 1,000 of his closest friends. Seneca was not only a Stoic philosopher but a statesman, dramatist, and humorist.

When he was 66 years old, Seneca requested an audience with Nero and sought to be relieved of his public duties due to his old age. Seneca then quietly retired to his country estates, seldom visiting Rome. Three years later, when he was 69 years old, Nero accused Seneca of being involved in a plot to kill the emperor and ordered Seneca to kill himself.

Seneca severed several veins to try to bleed to death. The blood loss was slow, and his was not a quick death. He tried to take poison, but that did not work either. Finally, his friends carried him to a bathtub so he could steam the room and suffocate.[13] He had enjoyed great power and wealth, but even when he was forced to commit suicide, he was fully present. As a Stoic, he was not afraid of death.

All through his life, Seneca relied on Stoic philosophy for resilience and strength. He was an excellent writer and wrote many letters to his friends and acquaintances.

These letters were rhetorical essays on Stoicism. Although many works (such as tragedies and drama) are attributed to him, the works of interest to us are those that include a dozen philosophical essays, and one hundred and twenty-four letters dealing with moral issues.

Epictetus, the slave with no name

Epictetus was born c. 55 CE in Hierapolis (present day Pamuk-kale, Turkey). Epictetus means "slave" or "acquired." We don't know what name his parents gave him or even whether they named him at all. It is said that his parents sold him to Epaph-roditos, a wealthy freedman, and secretary to Nero. Epictetus was lame. According to some accounts, Epaphroditos broke both Epictetus' legs for no reason. In any case, the lame Epicte-tus spent his youth as a slave in Rome.

Even as a slave, Epictetus was found to be gifted, so Epaphroditos sent him to study with the famous Stoic philoso-pher Musonius Rufus. It might sound illogical that the slave master who is reputed to have had Epictetus' legs broken would send him to study philosophy. However, it was not unusual dur-ing that period for a slave master to brag about his slaves being philosophers or masters of some other subject.

Eventually, Epictetus became a free man, but we don't know exactly how. After he had gained his freedom, Epictetus began to teach his philosophy. But not for long.

Around 93 CE, Emperor Domitian banished all philoso-phers from Rome. Epictetus fled to Nicopolis in Greece where he founded his philosophy school and remained until his death around 135 CE.

Although he left no writings of his own, his disciple Flavius Arrian faithfully transcribed the teachings of Epictetus. He col-lected them into eight books called *Discourses,* only four of which survive today. In addition, Arrian also captured a summary of Epictetus' teaching in a small manual called *Enchiridion*[14] (Handbook).

Marcus Aurelius, the Emperor inspired by a slave

Roman Emperor Marcus Aurelius was born in Rome in 121 CE into a wealthy and politically prominent family. He was a dedicated student of Latin and Greek and Stoicism. His teacher Rusticus introduced him to the teachings of Epictetus which had a great deal of influence on the young Marcus.

Emperor Hadrian arranged for his adopted son, Pius Antoninus, to adopt Marcus Aurelius. Around the age of 17, Marcus Aurelius became the son of Antoninus. He worked alongside his adopted father while learning the ways of government and public affairs.

In 140, Aurelius became Consul, the leader of the Senate. Over the years, he received more powers and responsibilities, and he became a strong source of counsel for Antoninus. He married Faustina, the Emperor's daughter, in 145, and had many children.

After his adoptive father died in 161, Aurelius rose to power. Unfortunately for Aurelius, his tenure was marked by war, treachery, and disease. He battled with the Parthian empire for control over lands in the East. Returning soldiers brought some type of disease back with them to Rome, which lingered for years and wiped out an estimated five million.[15]

After the Parthian War had ended, Aurelius faced military conflict with German tribes that crossed the Danube River and attacked a Roman city. Aurelius and his brother Verus fought the invaders. Verus died in 169, so Aurelius assumed the full responsibility for the battle. In 175, after hearing a rumor about Aurelius being deathly ill, Avidius Cassius proclaimed himself as the Emperor. As Aurelius traveled to the East to regain control, Cassius was murdered by his own soldiers. Subsequently, Aurelius toured the eastern provinces with his wife who died during this time. Marcus Aurelius died in 180.

While he was away in battles, Marcus Aurelius kept a personal diary, commonly known as "To Himself" or "Meditations." Not meant for publication, the journal contained the Emperor's Stoic musings written under difficult circumstances. Fortunately for us, it was found and later published. It contains some of the finest writings on Stoicism written by a practitioner.

There you have it. A lame slave with no name, a wealthy royal advisor who lived in luxury, and a Roman emperor who was inspired by a slave. Their lives and fortunes could not have been more different. They were among the least and the most powerful people in Rome, perhaps in the world, at that time. Their trials and tribulations were hardly similar. Yet all three practiced the same Stoic philosophy of freedom and happiness and fully participated in the festival of life. What they taught has been a source of inspiration for two thousand years and continues to be so to this day. The philosophy that endured

2,000 years is so relevant today that its principles are taught in the army.

Stoicism today

Over the centuries Stoicism continued to appeal to those who encountered it. It inspired several prominent heads of state and politicians like Frederick the Great, Benjamin Franklin, Theodore Roosevelt, Bill Clinton; writers like Dante, poets like Alexander Pope, Johann Wolfgang Goethe, and Matthew Arnold; thinkers like John Stuart Mill. In the recent past, it fell into disuse by the general public for three reasons.

One, the word *stoicism* came to mean something very different than the philosophy of Stoicism. For example, the dictionary definition of a stoic is, "a person who can endure pain or hardship without showing their feelings or complaining." This gives the impression that a Stoic is a long-suffering joyless person bravely facing his problems. When we talk about Stoic philosophy, this is not what we mean. As we shall see, a Stoic does not bravely endure hardships – she does not face hardships to begin with. What others see as problems, a Stoic does not. She knows how to deal with them.

Two, classical education has been by and large abandoned in schools and along with it philosophies like Stoicism.

Three, academic philosophers in recent times seem to have become more preoccupied in defining what a term means, such as, "What is the precise meaning of the term 'the good life'?" than with answering substantive questions such as, "How do we achieve the good life?" It is not uncommon today to obtain a PhD in philosophy without even having a passing familiarity with the influential philosophy of Stoicism. Factors such as these contribute to people not being exposed to Stoicism.

While academic philosophers seem to have largely abandoned Stoicism, others, especially psychologists, have discovered its principles and their relevance to modern life. Two influential modern psychotherapy methods – Rational Emotive Behavior Therapy (REBT) introduced by Albert Ellis and Cognitive Behavior Therapy (CBT) introduced by Aaron T. Beck – explicitly drew inspiration from Stoic principles. You can also find the influence of Stoicism on modern psychology, especially in Positive Psychology founded by high-profile social psychologists such as Martin Seligman and Mihaly Csikszentmihalyi.

The University of Exeter in England is actively propagating Stoicism with its Stoic Week and several free online courses. Stoicon (like Comicon, although Stoicon participants do not go around dressed like Stoic philosophers) is now being celebrated every year in different cities of the world. The National Health Service in the UK is experimenting with a philosophical toolkit for people facing serious illness. The US Army teaches the principles of Stoicism to soldiers. There are even a few novels in recent years inspired by Stoicism such as Tom Wolfe's *A Man in Full*[16] and Morgan Wade's *The Last Stoic*[17]. There are also several blogs, and Stoic get-togethers in different parts of the world.

What did the Stoics know that we don't?

Why all this interest in Stoicism? What did the Stoics know about personal freedom that we don't? They knew that, "no great equipment should be necessary for happiness... External things are of very little importance."[18] They taught us that you can be completely free if you live according to nature. You can be free no matter what. It doesn't matter if you are rich or poor, healthy or ill, young or old, educated or uneducated, have power or have no power. So how do we live according to nature so we can live in complete freedom?

WHAT THE STOICS KNEW

Some things in our life are under our complete control, and others are not. Things under our complete control are what we believe, what we desire or hate, and what we move toward or avoid. Other things are not in our complete control.

We can be free and happy by controlling only what is in our total control.

We should aim for a rational life which can also be termed as "life according to nature" or a "virtuous life." For the Stoics, virtue means wisdom (resourcefulness and discretion), justice (honesty), courage, and moderation. A person who lives rationally would be wise, just, courageous, and moderate.

We should avoid a life that is not according to reason, a life that includes vices: foolishness, injustice, cowardice, intemperance, and the rest.

Whatever is not under our total control is not necessary for our freedom. They are indifferents.

If things are under our partial control, we can pursue them if they are desirable indifferents, as long as we remember that they are not under our control.

We should enjoy whatever life offers us but shouldn't chase after things.

PART II

BE FREE

Be free of worries, anxieties, and problems

CHAPTER 3

Be Free to
Enjoy Every Sandwich

*I have to die? If it is now, then I will die now; if later, then I will have
my lunch now, since the hour for lunch has arrived – and dying I
will tend to later.*

Epictetus[19]

W hat is unshakable freedom? It is freedom that does
not depend on what other people do or think. It is
not decided by the amount of money you have or
don't have. It is not affected by what happens to
you or does not happen to you in your life. It does not require
that you achieve anything. It does not even matter if you are going to die soon or live for a long time.

How do you attain unshakable freedom? By controlling
what is under your control. A sailor does not control the wind.

Complaining about the wind does not make the wind go away but makes the sailor miserable and ineffective. By trying to control the wind, the sailor fails to control the sails. No matter how bad the wind, you can control only the sails.

This is so about everything we face. You can only control what is under your control. Either something is in our control or not. If we are to be sure of achieving freedom, by definition it should come from what is under our control. We are not free because we fail to make this most basic distinction.

What is not in your control is neither good nor bad. It is just the way it is; it is reality. You cannot reject reality without feeling trapped. Whatever you choose to think about reality, it is not under your control. When it rains, you cannot stop it. But if you don't want to get wet, you can carry an umbrella. If your thinking is "in accordance with nature" you cannot be hindered by anyone. You are free, and you will blame no one.

What is "in accordance with nature"? It is accepting reality simply because nature provides no alternative. There is no point in arguing with reality. Reality has a track record of winning all of the time. No exceptions.

But nature has also provided us with a weapon to counter the "negative" effects of reality on us. It is our ability to think rationally and to choose our thoughts.

This seemingly simple principle is the basis of unshakable freedom.

We have talked about many people who lived this way. We saw how Agrippinus continued to enjoy his workout, his bath, and his lunch while he was being tried and convicted. How Seneca faced his death. How Rhonda Cornum came out of her ordeal without being crushed by it. How Viktor Frankl felt free in a concentration camp amidst degradation and death. How James Stockdale survived more than seven years of incarceration and torture. So we know it is possible to have unshakable freedom. People have lived it, and it is no empty philosophy. Stoicism delivers on its promise of freedom.

Wisdom to know the difference

So if you are seeking freedom and happiness you have to be very clear about what is under your control and what is not. Reinhold Niebuhr summarized this in a serenity prayer in just 25 words: "God, grant me the serenity to accept the things I cannot change, Courage to change the things I can, And wisdom to know the difference."

You don't even need to ask God for "wisdom to know the difference." Epictetus very clearly spells out what is under your control and what is not.

Here is what is not under your control: Your body, your life, your possessions, relationships, wealth, fame, and reputation. You may object and say, "But I do have control over them! For example, I keep myself healthy." To be sure, you have *some* control over these things. You can have a healthier body by eating better and exercising; you can care for and insure your possessions; you can nurture your relationships; you can build your health, fame, and reputation. The Stoics would say that unless you have absolute control over these, you don't have control. You may unexpectedly become a victim of cancer or be hit by a car. Your possessions can be stolen, your investments may tank, your spouse may leave you, and your reputation can take a beating.

So if you don't have absolute control, you don't have control. If you are healthy, enjoy being healthy and preserve your health however you can, but don't be surprised and become bitter if you were to lose it. Your body, your life, your possessions, relationships, wealth, fame, and reputation are given to you. Enjoy the festival of life as long as it lasts and care for what you have been given as long as you have it, but do not lament their passing. Think of what you have as loans and when the time comes to return them, just do so. You don't have the choice not to return them anyway.

The brilliance of the Stoics

The brilliance of the Stoics is the very clear dichotomy they devised between what you can control and what you cannot. They said if something is only partially under your control, it is not under your control. This is a crucial point.

Many situations in life are such that, when we have partial control, we don't know exactly how much control we have. At what point do we discontinue our attempt to control? If we discontinue our attempt to control, have we given up too easily? If we continue, are we persisting when in reality we cannot succeed? Thus we get into a conflict with ourselves.

Even more than that, in some strange way, when we have partial control, we start believing we have total control. As Lee Lipsenthal points out, "At some irrational level, we believe that if we eat right, exercise daily, and take vitamins, we won't die. Although these actions may decrease our risk of illness, they give us a false sense of safety."[20] As a result, when things go wrong we might start feeling helpless because what we thought was under our control is not.

Clearly, only when we concentrate on what is under our total control can we be certain that we can achieve freedom. If we depend on things that are under our partial control, there is no guarantee that we will succeed. The goal of Stoics was the achievement of total freedom, not conditional freedom. For this reason, they did not leave something outside the dichotomy and ask God to provide the "wisdom to know the difference," between what they could change and what they could not. Stoics defined it.

And it is no tragedy that many things are not under our total control, either. We assume that the things not in our control, such as external objects and circumstances, are the most important things in our life. When we start losing control over them, as is inevitable, we experience grief, fear, envy, desire, anger, and anxiety. We feel we are not free. All this arises from the mistaken belief that freedom can be found outside of us. Once we understand that this is not the case, external things cease to affect us.

But can we still be free when so many things are not under our control? Yes, say the Stoics.

How?

By controlling the things that are under our control.

What are they?

Only three things: our *desires* (attraction or aversion), *judgments* (for or against) and *movement* (toward or away). Over these, we have full control. Nothing else. The window of control we have may appear small but is large enough to lead us to total freedom.

We are conditioned by society, by the media, and by other sources to believe that happiness comes from acquiring money, education, approval of others, fame, and other things. So how can we be happy without external things? How can we be free when things don't go our way?

The Stoic would say that external things are a part of reality, and therefore they are neither good nor bad. Since we don't control them, we should be indifferent to them. External things are givens, and we find freedom and happiness using what is under our control. As Epictetus put it, "It's not what happens to you, but how you react to it that matters."[21]

Here you are, stuck in traffic. You are already late. You did not create the traffic. Even if you are in some way responsible for being there at that time, you are already in it.

So traffic is a given. It is there as part of current reality. You have only two choices. You can go through the imagined consequences of your being late in your mind over and over again and feel miserable. You can blame public works, the accident, drivers who don't know how to drive, the weather, or whatever you think caused the delay, and feel agitated. Or you can use this gift of time to listen to music, plan your day, or simply relax. Either way, the traffic is going to be there, and you are going to be late. Your being imprisoned by negative thoughts and anger is not decided by the traffic, but by what you choose to think.

Death, be not proud

You can make this idea work whether the situation is trivial, like being stuck in traffic, or serious, like having cancer and a prognosis of only a few months to live.

That was exactly what happened to the musician Warren William Zevon. In the year 2000, he released a prophetically titled album *Life'll Kill Ya*, containing the song "Don't Let Us Get Sick." Well, your health is not under your control. Shortly before playing at the Edmonton Folk Festival in 2002, he started feeling dizzy, developed a chronic cough, and was diagnosed with mesothelioma.

What were his choices? He could have felt sorry for himself and spent his remaining days in fear. Instead, he began recording his final album, *The Wind*, and invited his friends Bruce Springsteen, Don Henley, Jackson Browne, Timothy B. Schmidt, Joe Walsh, David Lindley, Billy Bob Thornton, Emmylou Harris, Tom Petty, Dwight Yoakam, and others to participate. He continued to maintain his caustic sense of humor, even as his health kept deteriorating.

Later the same year, Zevon appeared on the *Late Show* with David Letterman. Letterman asked him what he had learned in the process of dying. Zevon replied, "I learned to enjoy every sandwich."

Zevon was told that his illness was terminal, but he continued to live as well as he could. Months after his diagnosis, he saw the birth of twin grandsons in June 2003 and the release of *The Wind* on August 26, 2003. He died two weeks later.

Among other things, Zevon's declaration, "enjoy every sandwich," inspired Lee Lipsenthal, a California physician dying of cancer in 2011, when he was facing his own mortality. Lee described his journey from the diagnosis and his eventual passing and published it under the title, *Enjoy Every Sandwich.* Lipsenthal wrote, "Pay attention to the good stuff that happens every day and enjoy what is, not what should have been or what might be. Enjoy every sandwich. My life is a sandwich, and I might as well savor every bite."[22]

Epictetus said, "There is only one way to happiness and that is to cease worrying about things which are beyond the power of our will."[23] Zevon's terminal illness was beyond his will. But his decisions to enjoy every sandwich and put together a final album with his friends were not. By choosing to enjoy every sandwich over fearful final months, he died free of fear. This is unshakable freedom. It is open to us all.

THE BIG IDEA 1
Problems are only problems
if you believe they are.

"Put away the belief, 'I've been wronged,' and with it will go the feeling. Reject your sense of injury and the injury itself disappears." Marcus Aurelius[24] What happens to you in life is not under your control. How you want to react to it is. By concerning yourself only with what is under your control, you can achieve personal freedom. Learn to enjoy every sandwich.

Suggestions for practicing the big idea

We often react in the way we are conditioned to. When we are upset, we become angry. We think this is a natural reaction, and we have no choice in the matter. In fact, people go as far as claiming that negative emotions are their "right." When people get ill, they take it personally and wonder, "Why me?" You hear people say, "I have a right to be angry and upset."

Yes, you do but you pay a price. The price is your freedom. Remember all negative emotions such as fear, anger, despair, and a sense of entitlement deprive us of our freedom by taking over our ability to think and act freely. There are two techniques we could use to overcome knee-jerk reactions and take back our freedom: the Pause-and-Examine technique and the Impersonal Projection technique.

1. The Pause-and-Examine Technique

If something happens to disturb your peace and you are about to be in the grips of frustration or anger, pause for a few seconds and take the steps outlined here.

Suppose you are faced with something unpleasant. It could be anything, such as a health problem, financial problem, or a relationship problem. You feel that some negative emotion is about to take you over.

Don't react immediately. Realize it may not be what your emotions say it is and you are reacting to what appears to be a negative situation. Take a close look at whatever is upsetting you. What appears to be negative may not be negative. Appearances can be deceptive. Say, "Appearance, wait for me a while. Let me see who you are, and what you represent. Let me test you." For example, you are angry with someone, and you want to get back at them. You don't immediately act on it but pause for a while to examine your emotion.

Appearances are deceptive. The appearance is telling you a story and painting a rosy picture of acting on negative emotions. For example, if you are angry with someone, your emotions could be telling you that you would be "taken for granted" unless you retaliate. You do not have to believe the story.

If you are seriously ill, you may feel depressed and ask, "Why me?" Realize that it is beyond your control to decide who gets sick. Instead, examine the event. What happens to your body is not under your total control.

Replace your negative thoughts with more positive ones that are in line with your freedom. For example, replace your angry thoughts with thoughts like, "I cannot control other people. Being angry only takes away my freedom to be happy without accomplishing anything. I would rather be free and happy than be angry."

Instead of being depressed about your illness you may say to yourself, "Illnesses are a natural part of living. There is no need to get upset. There might be cures for your illness. There are still ways to enjoy life no matter what happens."

If you keep practicing this way whenever something upsets you, eventually such discipline will become a trifling task for you, and nothing more. It may require constant practice, but as Epictetus reminds us, "The struggle is great, the task divine, to win a kingdom, to win freedom, happiness, to win serenity of mind."

This is quite doable, but we need to practice the technique over and over again. Remember, how people like Rhonda Cornum, James Stockwell, Warren Zevon, and Lee Lisenthal, who faced death and degradation, refused to react like most people would, but chose acts that are consistent with their freedom? With practice, we can do that too.

---

2. The Impersonal Projection technique

Things that happen to us are impersonal. Yet we take them personally. We look after ourselves well and yet develop an illness. Our reaction is, "Why me?" Our train is late. We feel that *our* train shouldn't be late. Yet, in all such cases, there is nothing personal. What happened just happened. The illness did not come specifically looking for us. The train would have been late whether it was our train or not. We intuitively know this – except when it happens to us.

If the same things happened to other people, we wouldn't give it a second thought. Instead, we would assume it was a natural sequence of events. If a stranger had contracted a disease, we wouldn't think, "Why her?", but rather say that it is unfortunate she got it; if a neighbor's cup broke, we would think, "It's no big deal. Accidents do happen." If you saw someone busily texting who, while walking, bumped into another person, you would probably hardly notice it. In none of these cases would we think that the event had something personal to do with the person involved. The Impersonal Projection technique makes use of this aspect of our thinking. Here is how it works:

You are faced with something you don't like. For example, you suddenly fall ill, someone is rude to you, or miss an opportunity to buy an investment.

As you are about to get upset (or even after that), take a moment to calm yourself and imagine that it happened to someone you don't know very well. You would, of course, sympathize with her, but you would also realize that it is a normal occurrence, nothing to be too upset or too worried about.

When you project your problem to another person, you might realize that what happened is not a terrible tragedy but what happens naturally in day-to-day life.

For a complete description of these two techniques see chapter 14, Stoics and Mental Fitness.

CHAPTER 4

Be Free of the Past

All the happiness you are seeking by such long, roundabout ways,
you can have it all right now ... if you leave all the past behind you.

Marcus Aurelius[25]

reedom is simple. If we look at anything that happens in our life, it falls into one of two categories. We have total control over it or we don't. If it is not under our total control, it is none of our concern. What is under our full control is enough for us to achieve freedom.

What about the past? Many people believe that their past binds them. What if you were mistreated by your parents? What if you were sexually abused? What if your family had been so dysfunctional that it still affects you? What if you were so underprivileged that you didn't get the right type of education, and your opportunities now are limited? Doesn't what happened in the past imprison you? Isn't there an army of professionals, from psychoanalysts to repressed memory specialists, who say so?

Stoics point out that the past cannot hinder you. Your past is over, and you have absolutely no control over it now. It has no control over you either, unless you let it. Whether you had a good childhood or a bad childhood, whether you were born privileged or not, whether you spent your time well or squandered it – none of these things are now under your control.

What about something that just happened? You missed your flight. You broke your favorite cup a minute ago. No matter. Once something has happened, you cannot change it. The past is a part of reality and immutable. They are the givens that you work with. They are, in Stoic terminology, "indifferents." You can train yourself to ignore indifferents. They are not needed for your freedom and happiness.

Because the past is an "indifferent," you are free of it. You are released from its hold. No matter what happened in the past, you are free of it. Your freedom has nothing to do with your past. Seneca asks, "What's the point of dragging up sufferings that are over, of being miserable now because you were miserable then?"[26]

Simple as this may sound, this is not how we live our lives. Our lives are full of regrets for the things we did or did not do; for the opportunities we missed; and for "what could have been." These are the things we have no control over and by thinking about them over and over again, we forego the freedom we have at this moment to act. By concentrating on what we have no control over, we lose sight of what we do have control over and thus give up the freedom to act in our own best interest.

The janitor and the class of 2012

There was something different about Honors student, Gac Filipaj, than his fellow Columbia University graduates in 2012. The fact that he was an immigrant from Eastern Europe? No, that is not that unusual. The fact that he was 52 while the average age of the graduating class was around 20? Perhaps somewhat unusual, but not unheard of. Could it be that, at the time he graduated, he was a janitor at the university? A 52-year-old immigrant janitor graduating with honors from an Ivy League school? Now *that* was unusual.

Twenty years earlier, in 1992, Gac, an ethnic Albanian, left Montenegro and fled the Yugoslav republic that was facing a brutal civil war. He was about to be drafted into the Yugoslavian army which meant he had to fight Albanians. Not wanting to do that, he fled Yugoslavia, even before he completed his schooling. He managed to get into the US and get a job as a janitor, mopping floors, taking out trash, and cleaning toilets.

Well, if you are an immigrant janitor when you are forty with scant knowledge of English you would assume that your past has worked against you, you are imprisoned by it, and there is not a lot you can do about it. But Gac was inspired by his reading of Seneca's letters. He left his past behind, did not worry about "indifferents", and aspired to have a simple, honest, honorable life, in the spirit of Seneca.

He soon found out that, as an employee of the university, he could study for free. But first, he had to attend English classes and learn English, which he did before starting to work on his degree. During the day, Gac worked the 2.30 – 11.00 pm shift, after which he would get back to his Bronx apartment and study late into the night. Prior to exams, he would work through the night. With a full-time job and having to attend classes during the day, it took him 12 years but eventually he graduated.

At the time of graduation, Gac was earning $22 an hour in his job as a janitor. He used that to support not only himself but his brother, sister-in-law, and two kids who lived back in in Montenegro, foregoing even common things such as a cellphone and a computer.

The past did not bind Gac. He was free of its hold over him. By the way, he is now hoping to complete his Master's and maybe his Ph.D. as well.

Gac ignored the "indifferents" and used what was in his power. This is Stoic freedom.

What the Stoic would applaud here is NOT Gac's success in getting a degree, praiseworthy as it may be. However, for Stoics, success is also an indifferent, not necessary for one's freedom. What is critical here is that he did not let the past hinder him in what he wanted to achieve. His lack of knowledge of English, his age, his position in life – none of these could hinder him. He was free of his past.

But if succeeding or failing are both "indifferents", why should he bother? He might as well not have toiled, worked late, and educated himself. He could have spent his money and time in bars and coffee houses having a relaxing time. Why did I even bother to bring up his story?

Stoics actually distinguish two types of indifferents: *preferred* indifferents and *dispreferred* indifferents. For example, health is an indifferent, because it is not within our control and is not necessary for our freedom and happiness. But if we had a choice, would we rather be healthy or sick? Healthy, of course. Being healthy then is a preferred indifferent. So, to increase our chances of being healthy, we use our ability to act such as exercising and eating right when they are within our power. But all the while we recognize even if our health fails, we will continue to be free.

Similarly, if we had a choice, would we prefer to be in an accident or not be in an accident? We would of course rather not get into an accident. Safety is a preferred indifferent then. So we drive with caution. However, if we did get into an accident, we would still keep our calm.

For Gac, obtaining an education was a preferred indifferent. So he worked towards that end. If he had failed to graduate, from a Stoic perspective, he would still be free of the past.

What we go after in life – things such as reputation, health, wealth, and education – are "indifferents" or "moral neutrals." For example, money is an indifferent, neither good nor bad, morally neutral. If you use the money to feed yourself, to feed your family, to support a charity, then it is "good," it is a preferred indifferent. But if you use the money to buy hard drugs or fund terrorism, then it is "bad," a dispreferred indifferent.

So it is with everything outside our total control. As Epictetus said, "'Being healthy is good; being is sick is bad?' No, my friend: enjoying health in the right way is good; making bad use of your health is bad."[27]

In the Stoic scheme of things the indifferents play an interesting role. Preferred indifferents provide us the means to use things that are not needed for our freedom. They can enhance our enjoyment of life. And yet they are not needed for our freedom and are not in our total control. So we can enjoy them as long as they are under our control and let them go without complaining when conditions change.

As Seneca pointed out, a wise man knows how to handle preferred indifferents. He neither seeks "fortune's bounty," nor rejects it, nor mourns its loss."[28] Stoics do not reject the world they live in. They are very much an active part of it while still being independent of whatever comes their way.

Madiba and his captors

Nelson Mandela is often referred to as a man who exhibited stoic qualities. We all know his well-documented story. Mandela studied to become a lawyer in his native South Africa. When the government introduced its apartheid policies, he fought against them. Initially, he was committed to nonviolent protest.

However, later on, he decided on leading a sabotage campaign along with the African National Congress (ANC) against the government. In 1962, he was arrested and tried. In his opening remark at his trial, Mandela admitted to some of the charges against him. He defended the ANC's actions and denounced the injustices of apartheid.

While concluding his comments he had this to say: "I have cherished the ideal of a democratic and free society in which all persons live together in harmony and with equal opportunities. It is an ideal which I hope to live for and to achieve. But if needs be, it is an ideal for which I am prepared to die." The trial ended with his conviction for conspiring to overthrow the state. He spent the next 27 years in different prisons – most famously on Robben Island, and also in Pollsmar and Victor Verster prisons.

While in prison, he was often in solitary confinement. Letters, books, and even regular visitors were strictly controlled by the authorities. His job in prison frequently included breaking rocks in a quarry. Mandela exercised vigorously every morning and organized protests when called for. While in prison, he had to endure the death of his mother and eldest son.

In the 1990s, as international pressure grew on the South African government, it also became clear that there might be a major racial war. As a result, President F.W. de Klerk released Nelson Mandela. Subsequently, he became the president of South Africa.

Mandela went into prison as a youthful 44-year-old and came out of it as an aging 71-year-old man. Remarkably, he came out a better man than he went in. While long prison sentences dehumanize many inmates, making them bitter and violent, Mandela used his prison time to cultivate his body and mind. It would have been natural for him to carry a grudge against his captors, who deprived him of freedom. It would have been easy for him to take revenge on his captors or the white people of South Africa. Instead, he left his past behind.

As I walked out the door toward the gate that would lead to my freedom, I knew if I didn't leave my bitterness and hatred behind, I'd still be in prison."

Nelson Mandela

When asked if he did not feel bitter and wanted to seek revenge against those who kept him for the past 27 years, his response was, "As I walked out the door toward the gate that would lead to my freedom, I knew if I didn't leave my bitterness and hatred behind, I'd still be in prison."

Bill Clinton, recalling his many meetings with Mandela, said that Mandela was, "the only free man I ever knew," who taught Clinton, "You simply cannot be free without forgiveness." This means leaving the past completely behind you.

Mandela's courage, willingness to face death if need be, and, above all, his ability to leave his past behind bearing no ill will against those who deprived him of his freedom for 27 years is another example of Stoicism in action.

Whether a janitor or a Madiba, the principle is the same

Nelson Mandela, reverentially referred to as Madiba (meaning "father" in Xhosa), is a well-known figure who changed the lives of millions of South Africans. Gac Filipaj, a little-known figure, changed only his life and perhaps a few others. And yet both used the same principle: treating the past as an indifferent and leaving it behind. This is the power of Stoic principles. They are universally applicable. They transcend time and the person. Stoic principles helped an emperor and a slave a long time ago; two thousand years later, they helped an unknown janitor and a well-known statesman.

THE BIG IDEA 2
Leave your past behind

"All the happiness you are seeking by such long, roundabout ways, you can have it all right now... if you leave all the past behind you ..." Marcus Aurelius[29]

You cannot change the past, no matter how recently or how far back something happened. What happened in the past or when it happened is not relevant to your freedom now. You are completely free at this moment, and you can choose things that are consistent with your freedom.

Suggestions for practicing the big idea

There are two visualization techniques you can practice to remind yourself to leave your past behind. The first one, the Sun Beam Visualization exercise, is constructed by extending an analogy used by Marcus Aurelius. The second is the South Indian Monkey Trap Visualization technique. The latter is inspired by Epictetus[30] who gave the analogy of children putting their hand into a narrow-necked jar to grab nuts and figs but were unable to pull their hands out but the actual technique itself comes from *Zen and the Art of Motorcycle Maintenance*[31] by Robert Pirsig. The imagery used by Pirsig is so powerful that it might be useful for us when trying to be free of the past.

1. The Sun Beam Visualization technique

You may want to practice this visualization when you feel you are trapped by your past, and there is no way out.

Sit down and relax. Imagine the sun pouring down its light in all directions. In front of you, there is a big wall. The sunlight cannot go through the wall. The sunlight does not clash with the obstruction but gently stops at the wall.

Imagine someone drilling the wall and creating a hole. Suddenly the sunlight starts passing through it. Imagine now that the wall is completely collapsed and the sun shines immediately on the other side of what was once an obstacle. The sunlight would react the same way whether the obstacle has been there for a minute or for one thousand years. The fact that the sunlight might have been obstructed by the wall for one thousand years does not stop it from going forward the moment the obstacle is removed.

Imagine that you are the sun and the sunbeam is your journey through life. The obstacles that stopped you from doing what you wanted to do are in your past. Your past is gone, so are the obstacles. Just as the sunlight is free to move forward the very moment the obstacle is gone, you are free to move forward the moment the past situation has changed.

Realize that to imagine that your past – bad childhood, poverty, broken home – is somehow holding you back is like the sunlight believing that it cannot go forward because it was obstructed so long. Contemplate living like the sun whose light moves forward the moment the obstacle is removed – your past does not have power over you unless you believe it does.

To liberally paraphrase Marcus Aurelius:

> [You] should make no violent or impetuous collision with the obstacles which are in your way; neither should you fall down when you meet an obstacle, but be fixed, and enlighten whoever receives you.[32]

2. The South Indian Monkey Trap
Visualization technique

When we imagine that we are trapped by the past – be it a dysfunctional family, impoverished childhood, or having had to face traumatic incidents – if we don't let go of the past, it may affect our future. How damaging this can be is illustrated by how monkeys are being caught in South India because they can't let go, even when their life is at stake.

The trap, which is attached to a stake, consists of a hollowed-out coconut with some rice inside. There is a hole large enough for the monkey to get its hand in but once it grabs the rice inside, its fist gets too large to come out. The villagers are coming to get the monkey. All that monkey needs to do is to open its fist, and it is free. Yet it won't. It doesn't realize that what is restraining it is not the trap itself, but its failure to see that it can simply free itself by releasing what is in its hand. It has trapped itself.

Whenever you believe that something in the past is holding you back, imagine yourself to be a monkey that is caught in the trap. The rice that you are holding on to is your past. Now you have a choice. You can hold on to your past like the monkey holding on to its rice, unwilling to let go. The result would be the same for you as it would be for the monkey: loss of freedom. Just as the monkey can simply release the rice and go free, you can let go of the past and go free. It's as simple as that. Let go of the past.

If you want to gain freedom, try to control what is under your control. Do not try to control what is not under your control. The past is not under your control. It is not controlling you either unless you believe it is. What you can do now *is* under your control. Let go of the past.

As Epictetus put it:

See children thrusting their hands into a narrow-necked jar, and striving to pull out the nuts and figs it contains: if they fill the hand, they cannot pull it out again, and then they fall to tears. "Let go a few of them, and then you can draw out the rest!"[33]

For a complete description of these two techniques see chapter 14, Stoics and Mental Fitness.

CHAPTER 5

Be Free of the Emotional Roller Coaster

If you will listen to me, wherever you are, and whatever you are do-
ing, you will not feel suffering, or anger, or compulsion, or hin-
drance, but you will pass your time without worries.

Epictetus[34]

W e work long hours, cope with unreasonable demands at work, shoulder family responsibilities,
and try to live within our means. Then we turn the
TV on and, wouldn't you know it, it's all bad news.
Floods, storms, tsunamis, some dictator trying to get hold of nu-
clear weapons, terrorists killing people indiscriminately, and so
on. All this creates a low level of mental unease and stress. A

mild free-floating anxiety, which we don't even recognize, pervades our lives. From time to time when something unpleasant happens, we explode outwardly and suffer mental anguish.

Our greatest threats to freedom in most parts of the modern world are not major disasters. No wild animal threatens us, no tyrant or despot can throw us in prison, kill us or exile us. There are institutions – however ineffective – to deal with catastrophic events such as tsunamis, mad cow disease, and so on. While catastrophes can strike us at any time, these are not everyday threats in the modern world, assuming that we live in a reasonably stable democracy. We may not live under utopian conditions, but most of us don't live in constant fear of losing life, limb, and property.

What imprisons us is the constant barrage of negative emotions generated by everyday events that are not to our liking. The toast is burnt, we are a little bit late, we just said the wrong thing, and someone did not see where they were going and bumped into us. Each such event annoys us but is trivial enough to go unnoticed. But cumulatively they take their toll. Dale Carnegie, who studied Stoic philosophers like Epictetus and Marcus Aurelius as a part of his project on how to stop worrying and start living, tells this story:

On the slope of Long's Peak in Colorado, three gigantic trees stood for four centuries. During this time they were struck by lightning fourteen times as well as by countless avalanches and storms. They withstood all these attacks. In the end, an army of thousands of beetles attacked the trees, ate their way through the bark, and slowly leveled the trees to the ground. Major disasters could not destroy these mighty trees, but an army of tiny beetles did.

We do not face major tragedies every day. But we face a lot of minor problems each day of our lives. The quality of our lives is decided by how we react to everyday events. We are stuck in traffic. We are upset with the other drivers, and with the lanes that are closed for maintenance. We spill coffee on our shirt. We are immediately upset and embarrassed. A friend shows up late causing us to miss the beginning of a movie. We are annoyed with the friend. We are forced to go to a show that we don't want to see because our spouse wants to and we feel miserable for a couple of hours. The supermarket line we are in happens to be the slowest moving one. We fume at the inefficient checkout clerk. Someone in the subway is rude to us when we are minding our own business, and we keep going over the incident in our minds for the rest of the day. These everyday emotions take their toll. At the end of the day, we are exhausted. How can we be free when we are surrounded by thoughtless, demanding, and inefficient people?

Stoics were well aware of our getting emotionally worked up by trivialities. Epictetus put it this way: "Don't grow peevish about trivialities. The vinegar is bad, it is sharp; the honey's bad, it upsets my constitution; I didn't like the vegetables."[35] In reality, what happens doesn't really upset us but what we think about what happens does.

Imagine if we decide to think differently. We spill coffee on our shirt. Instead of getting embarrassed we see how efficiently we can remove the stain. If the shirt is still stained, we don't have to keep thinking about it. After all, it is hardly an earth-shattering event to anyone else except for us (if we choose to make it so). Apart from us, for how many people does it really matter? Our friend shows up late causing us to miss the beginning of a movie. We may still be able to make sense of the movie and enjoy it without feeling agitated about missing the beginning. The line we happen to be in is the slowest moving one. Instead of fuming at the checkout clerk, we can plan the day, we can do some isometric exercises or simply relax and observe other people in the line. Someone is rude to us on the subway. Instead of going over that incident for the rest of the day, we decide not to let the hurt last longer than the incident itself. We can even choose to feel compassionate to the person who was rude to us. Maybe he had a rough day or something unfortunate had happened to him. Wouldn't a lot of our problems be non-problems if we thought this way?

We don't control most things that come our way during the day. Every time we resist what comes our way, we lose some of our freedom. People being rude. Trains being late. The guy is talking too loudly and too long on his cell phone in a quiet restaurant where you are having dinner. The person who cuts you off on the highway. Red wine spilled on your white carpet by a guest. No, we don't have any control over any of these. We don't even control our health 100%.

But just because we don't control these things, that does not mean they affect our ability to be free. We don't depend on what we cannot control. You may say, "Be careful that you don't get ill. It's bad." But Epictetus would respond that it is like saying, "Guard against ever entertaining the idea that three is equivalent to four. It's bad."[36] It doesn't change reality.

When it begins to sink in that anything external is just reality in which we exist, we realize we need to create our freedom within the framework of that reality. Just as water is the reality for a fish, whatever happens to us is reality to us. Just as a fish cannot escape water and still survive, we cannot resist reality and still be free. Once we clearly understand this, we are free to explore the resources available to us and choose a reaction to anything life presents us. We gain clarity to free ourselves from all emotional turmoil and begin to enjoy the freedom that flows out of it.

Be free of complaints

Many people have a tendency to complain even when things are good. Epictetus said of complainers: "Even when they are invited, they don't act as if they are on holiday, or play an appropriate part; instead they whine, they curse their fate, their luck, and their company. They don't appreciate what they have."[37]

Even when things do not go the way we expect them to there is no need to complain. What is not under our control is nothing to us. As we train ourselves to change the way we look at things over which we have no control, we will have fewer and fewer things to complain about. As we complain less and less, we will enjoy life more and more. As Epictetus said, "Do I have to go to Rome? Then I go to Rome. To Gyara? All right, I go to Gyara instead. To Athens? Then Athens it is. To jail? Then I go to jail."[38] When we do not resist reality and instead welcome it, we will have fewer and fewer things to be upset about or complain about. When we stop complaining – as a Stoic you would not find any reason to complain under any condition – our life becomes more and more of a festival. Therefore, "Let no one, not even yourself, ever hear you abusing the court life again."

THE BIG IDEA 3
Don't let the indifferents rob your freedom

"Take away your opinion and your complaint is gone. Take away the complaint, 'I have been harmed,' and your harm is gone." (Marcus Aurelius)[39]

Avoid having opinions on things that happen every day. You are not in charge of other people's behavior; they will act as they please. These are beyond your control and are "indifferents." They are a part of reality, neither good nor bad. Remember their true nature and decide the best way to respond to such situations that is consistent with our freedom.

Suggestions for practicing the big idea

Because of decades of conditioning, we react to minor annoyances with negative emotions that are out of proportion. Stoics suggest two techniques that, if practiced diligently, will release you from the grip of unpleasant emotions and restore your freedom.

1. The Two Handles technique

A way of looking at current frustrations is to realize that everything has two handles. One is compatible with freedom, and the other not compatible with freedom. Suppose your friend said something that was hurtful. The handle, "He hurt me," leads to anger and other negative consequences. When we are angry, we are in the clutches of a negative emotion and therefore not free. So this handle cannot be used here. The other handle, "My friend and I have shared many past experiences together. We have many things in common, he has forgiven me in the past, and he has done many good things for me, even if he has said something now that I think is hurtful," is better suited for the current situation.

When we use the second handle, we don't feel hindered by our friend or by our anger. When you are upset with your colleague, a response like "He is not very smart" or "He is stubborn" or "He is being unreasonable," is the incorrect handle. The handle, "I am grateful for his input. Let me understand this from his perspective," is likely to diffuse anger and likely to lead to a more pleasant interaction with your colleague.

By consistently using these techniques whenever we face everyday distress, we can gradually be free of their hold on us. As we practice, we will notice that everyday annoyances don't imprison us anymore. Remember the words of Epictetus:

Everything has two handles, the one by which it may be carried, the other by which it cannot. If your brother acts unjustly, don't lay hold on the action by the handle of his injustice for by that it cannot be carried; but by the opposite, that he is your brother, that he was brought up with you; and thus you will lay hold on it, as it is to be carried.[40]

2. Marcus' Nine technique

This technique is a little bit more detailed. While the Two Handles technique is a quick fix for dealing with everyday annoyances, the Marcus' Nine technique (devised by Marcus Aurelius) is more a step-by-step approach. It consists of four questions and five reminders. Whenever you are upset by someone, take time out and use the following 9 steps to diffuse emotional upsets. This technique is particularly helpful when you are deeply upset.

Marcus' Nine consists of four questions and five reminders:

Questions to yourself

Marcus' Q1. Diffuse hostility. *What is my relationship to this person?* Life works best when we cooperate with and serve each other. So don't approach the situation with hostility towards the other person.

Marcus' Q2. Understand why he/she is upsetting you. *Who is the person who is upsetting me?* Why do they behave this way? What makes them think that this is acceptable behavior? Don't prejudge the person, but try to understand why the person is behaving the way he or she does.

Marcus' Q3. Evaluate the situation calmly. *Are they right?* If they are right, we should not feel unhappy about it. If they are wrong, then they are acting out of ignorance. In either case, we don't have to react immediately.

Marcus' Q4. Be compassionate. *Don't I also do similar things that are wrong?* There is no need to judge the other person harshly. Even if you think that you are perfect and consider yourself above doing anything wrong, you are a human being like others. Do we always behave the way we should?

Reminders to yourself

Marcus' R1. Know that you cannot know the whole picture. *We cannot even know if the person is wrong* because we don't know the whole context. We don't know the other person's life and what events led up to his behaving this way.

Marcus' R2. Be aware that life's short. Don't spend it in vexation. *Our life is short.* We will all be soon dead. Why spend the short time we have on this earth in vexations and grievances?

Marcus' R3. Know that other people's opinions have no power to disgrace you. *If you choose not to be hurt by somebody's words or acts, you won't be hurt.* If the other person's acts are shameful, why should you waste your time thinking about them?

Marcus' R4. Know that your anger brings you pain. *What is hurting you is your anger and vexation about someone else's behavior.* By being angry, you bring pain to yourself long after the event that caused your anger is gone.

Marcus' R5. Be genuinely good. Don't fake it. *You are not genuinely being Stoic if all you do is to smile while being upset by the other people's actions.* Try to be of a genuinely pleasant disposition and not take offense at others' behavior, even if you would not act that way.

Marcus Aurelius who gave us this technique had this to say:

> *Remember these nine rules as if you have received them as a gift from the Muses and begin at last to be a man while you live.*[41]

For a complete description of these two techniques see chapter 14, Stoics and Mental Fitness.

CHAPTER 6

Be Free of Fear

Where fear is, happiness is not.

Seneca[42]

William Shakespeare, who is said to have had some Stoic influence says, "A coward dies a thousand times before his death, but the valiant taste of death but once. It seems to me most strange that men should fear, seeing that death, a necessary end, will come when it will come."[43] This is precisely the Stoic view. To the Stoic, death can come only once. She is not afraid to die. She knows it is inevitable. If she has to die now, so be it. But until she dies, for a Stoic, everything is normal.

Helvidius and the Emperor

Freedom is incompatible with fear. If you are afraid, you are not free. So a free person is a fearless person. Stoics admired people like the Roman senator Helvidius who defied Emperor Vespasian. Roman Emperor Vespasian was trying to dissuade Helvidius from attending a Senate meeting because the Emperor felt that Helvidius had views that contradicted that of the Emperor. Vespasian says to Helvidius[44]:

"Do not go in."

"Disqualify me as a senator if you want me not to go in. Otherwise, I must go in."

"Go in then, but do not give your opinion."

"I won't, if you don't call on me for my vote."

"But I must call on you for your vote."

"Then I must give my honest opinion."

"Give your opinion, and I will kill you."

"Kill me if you must, and I will die without flinching."

Freedom from fear shown by Helvidius is what Stoics value. When we are afraid, we are not free. Our mind freezes.

Real freedom is not for show. It is not a simple act of defiance. A Stoic doesn't want to show the world how strong she is. For a Stoic, what others think of her is an indifferent. But the Stoic knows that, to the extent you are fearful, you cannot be free.

Helvidius' defiance did not come from his desire to show how strong he was or his feeling superior to the Emperor. In fact, Helvidius was quite prepared to go away if the Emperor had chosen to remove him from the Senate. He even volunteered to keep quiet if he was not called for his vote.

The source of Helvidius' defiance of the Emperor comes from his realization that if he valued anything that is completely beyond his control, he would not be free. If he valued his life more than his freedom, anyone could threaten his life and force him to do anything. Stoics believed that ultimately your life is not under your control. You will die someday, no matter what. Not all your visits to the gym, not all your money, not all your spiritual practices, and not all your hopes can stop it. As Omar Khayyam[45] put it

The Moving Finger writes; and, having writ,
Moves on: nor all thy piety nor wit
Shall lure it back to cancel half a line,
Nor all thy tears wash out a word of it.

Helvidius knew that if he agreed to the Emperor's unreasonable demand, he could make more and more unreasonable demands because he (Helvidius) always would be fearful of losing his life. If he refused to accede to the Emperor's demand, he had two choices: speak up and likely be killed or shut up and live. To Helvidius, speaking up at the risk of being killed was far more preferable to leading a fearful life.

It is this type of Stoic fearlessness that led Mahatma Gandhi some 2000 years later to defy the mighty British totally unarmed.

Gandhi and the British might

When Gandhi was arrested and charged with sedition by the British, although he was a British-trained lawyer, he did not defend himself. Instead, he pleaded guilty but held that the law under which he was being tried was evil, and therefore he had to defy it. This is what he had to say to his tormentors (like Helvidius said to the Emperor 2,000 years earlier):

"I am... here to invite and submit to the highest penalty that can be inflicted upon me for what in law is a deliberate crime and what appears to me to be the highest duty of a citizen. The only course open to you, the judge, is either to resign your post and dissociate yourself from evil, if the law you called upon to administer is an evil, and therefore I am innocent; or to inflict me the severest penalty."[46]

To Helvidius, and Gandhi, imprisonment or even death meant nothing because they were totally unafraid. People could take away their body and physically confine them to a cell, but their spirit was unbowed and free. This is Stoic freedom. (While Gandhi himself was not a follower of formal Stoicism, he had read the Stoics while he was in prison between 1922 and 1924 following the trial and agreed with much of what Stoics had to say. In his 2012 book *Gandhi and the Stoics*[47], Richard Sorabji explores how closely Gandhi's thoughts and actions resembled those of Stoics in so many ways.)

The teenager and the terrorist

On an afternoon in October 2012, a fifteen-year-old girl boarded her school bus in northwestern Pakistan. A gunman followed her asking for her by name, pointed a gun at her and shot her three times at point blank range. Her crime? She wanted to go to school despite the edict of the Taliban prohibiting women from seeking formal education. One of the bullets traveled under her skin across her face and went into her shoulder. Malala – that's her name – remained unconscious and in critical condition several days after that. Miraculously, she survived.

When she regained consciousness and recovered from the shots that could have easily killed her, she wasn't afraid. She became an even more vocal advocate for women's right to education. In 2014, at the age of 17, she became the youngest person ever to receive the Nobel Prize.

Malala harbored no anger against the person who shot her. On the *Daily Show* she said that, after she had regained consciousness, she was wondering what she would do if a Talib came again looking for her. She first told herself, "Throw a shoe at him," but then she said to herself, "No, if I did that, I would be no better than the Talib. I would tell him that he is mistaken. All I need is education and so do his children. I will tell him 'That's all I have to say. Now you do whatever you want.'"

It is unlikely that the fifteen-year-old Malala was aware of Stoic philosophy when she was shot in 2012, but she exhibited stoic qualities as strongly as any Stoic ever did.

When she said that, "The terrorists thought they would change my aims and stop my ambitions, but nothing changed in my life except this: weakness, fear, and hopelessness died. Strength, power, and courage were born," she stood as a living proof of the sentiments expressed by Marcus Aurelius 2,000 years ago: "Mind converts every hindrance to its activity into an aid and so that which is a hindrance is made furtherance to an act; and that which is an obstacle on the road helps us on this road."[48]

When she refused to be drawn into violence herself, she was echoing this sentiment of Marcus Aurelius: "The best way of avenging yourself is not to become like the wrongdoer."[49]

When she faced death without flinching, she became a shining example of what Epictetus had said, "One way to guarantee freedom is to be ready to die."[50]

Her freedom from anger and resentment against her attacker is another expression of the Stoic attitude, similar to the one expressed by Helvidius when threatened by the Emperor.

Fearlessness in our daily lives

How would we apply this in our daily lives? After all, we don't face the imminent threat of someone killing us or imprisoning us for a long time for our beliefs. An everyday equivalent would be your boss asking you to do something you don't like personally. If you were to tell your boss that you would not do it, and she may fire you if she wished, it would be a simple act of defiance. It would be more an act of stupidity (unless it violates some ethical principle you hold dear) rather than of fearlessness. Since you are paid to do your job, it is your duty to do what is asked of you.

Stoics were clear on this point. For example, Marcus Aurelius did not care for the violent gladiatorial games. Yet, as a Roman emperor, he felt it was his duty to be at gladiatorial sports. So, setting aside his personal views, he attended such events. One should do one's duties, however one feels about them.

Helvidius defied the emperor at the risk of losing his life because he believed that, as a senator, it was his duty to speak up if he was called upon to vote, not because he felt a great urge to speak up. He was prepared to go away, if he was relieved of his duties as a senator. Similarly, Gandhi defied the British Empire because he believed that, as a citizen, it was his duty to disobey the law that he perceived to be evil.

So the modern equivalent of fearlessness would not be mindlessly rejecting what you don't like to do or indulging in pointless defiance. Rather, you would cooperate with others and do your duties as far as possible, even if they appeared unreasonable to you. However, fear of losing your job will not stop you from speaking up if it involves doing something unethical from your perspective or doing something harmful to others. Fear would not stop you from doing the right thing.

THE BIG IDEA 4
Where there is fear, freedom is not

Epictetus said, "One way to guarantee freedom is to be ready to die."[51] We forego freedom when we are afraid. It leads us to do things that are not in line with the good life. Because a Stoic values mental freedom above physical freedom, he is not afraid.

Suggestions for practicing the big idea

Fear arises when we feel helpless and overwhelmed by the current situation. People like Helvedius, Gandhi, and Malala saw themselves as a small instrument in a greater cause: freedom for themselves and others. We develop fearlessness when we become completely aware that certain things are not under our control and, since we can achieve freedom with what we can control, we are not afraid of anything that is not under our control.

In reality, the fear we face every day is not about severe things like death or imprisonment. Our fears are about our jobs, possessions, future, people we are close to, people we think can harm us. We can train ourselves be less fearful of everyday insecurities by using the two techniques described below: The Cosmic View technique and the Entitlement Challenge technique.

1. The Cosmic View technique

This technique is useful whenever you get into a difficult situation that might even seem hopeless. When we face a fearful situation, we see it in close-up. This exaggerates its impact. We feel we are permanently trapped. Yet nothing lasts forever. Not even our misfortune. Everything is constantly changing. One way to get rid of that fear is to see it in a much larger context. If a situation seems impossible and you feel fearful, relax and view everything with a different perspective.

Sit in a comfortable position and take a few deep breaths. Image you are on a space ship so far above the earth that the planet looks like a giant globe. Try to locate yourself on this globe. You are nothing more than a speck, too small to be seen. Realize whatever happens to you is trivial in the larger scheme of things. You have the resources to cope with whatever happens. Even if you make a mistake, it does not matter. Everything will change soon anyway.

Think of the fourteen billion years that went before you appeared on this earth and the several billion years that will come after you are gone. As you see your problems in the larger context, whatever you are facing is not as severe as it looked and surely it is within your power to adjust to whatever happens. Even if you make a mistake, everything will soon change and be gone forever anyway.

Move forward in time and imagine what you worried would happen had already happened. See that you have not collapsed under its weight. It is never as bad as you imagine and, even if it is, you have the resources to cope with it.

Look back into your life. How many things that you were afraid of five years ago can you even remember? Of those things you remember, how many came to pass? Fear makes us worry about our reputation, our losing what we have, our getting what we don't want, and so on.

When we view it from the cosmic perspective, we see all these things mean very little, and we can go on with our life without any of the things we are afraid of losing. We don't have to be afraid of anything. The vision will wash away the dust of fear enveloping you.

As Marcus Aurelius said:

> You should view earthly things as if you viewed them from some higher place: assemblies, armies, agriculture labors, marriages, treaties, births, deaths, noise of the courts of justice, desert places ... a mixture of all things and an orderly combination of contraries.[52]

2. The Entitlement Challenge technique

We feel that we are entitled to many good things in life: a good job, an attractive spouse, investments that do well, and so on. When we get them, we develop a fear of losing the things we think we are entitled to. We could lose our job, our spouse, and our investments. This insecurity makes us anxious and we impulsively do things that are not in our long-term interest.

The fact is, we are not entitled to anything. Why should we be? Suppose you are afraid that you will not get a job. The fear arises because you believe you are somehow entitled to get the job. You are afraid of the stock market crashing because you think you are entitled to your investments going up. If you are afraid your loved one may die, you believe you are entitled to your loved ones not dying. Yet as a matter of reality we are not entitled to any of these things.

So whenever you feel you did not get something you wanted, do not feel angry or disappointed. Instead challenge your emotions and ask, "Why do I think I am *entitled* to this?" When we challenge our feeling of entitlement often enough, we will start feeling grateful for what we have rather than being fearful of what might happen.

This is how Epictetus[53] put it:

> *"But he is a bad father.'*
>
> *"Well, have you any natural claim to a good father? No, only to a father."*
>
> *"My brother wrongs me."*
>
> *"Do not consider what he does, but what you must do if your purpose is to keep in accord with nature."*

For a complete description of these two techniques see chapter 14, Stoics and Mental Fitness.

CHAPTER 7

Be free of future anxieties

Don't let the future cause you anxiety, for the future will arrive in its own good time, and you will have the same mind that you use now to deal with the present.

Marcus Aurelius[54]

We cannot predict the future. It is not within our power to do so. Because things and people are impermanent, we are often in a state of insecurity about what might happen in the future. That does not stop us from worrying about the many bad things that might happen to us.

A practicing Stoic would say that there is absolutely nothing to worry about because no amount of worry can change the course of events. So he would not fill his mind with hypotheticals such as:

- What would happen if I lost my job?
- What would happen if I missed this flight?

- What would happen if my spouse left me?
- What would happen if I didn't have enough money to retire?
- And so on.

For a Stoic, freedom does not depend on what happens outside of oneself. You will always have the resources to cope with whatever happens to you. This knowledge sets you free.

Worrying is not the same as planning

> *My life has been filled with terrible misfortunes; most of which never happened.*
>
> Michel de Montaigne (1544 – 1592)

Being anxious about the future is not the same as planning and acting. A person who is concerned about missing a flight would plan to leave home early. This is planning, not worrying. But once you are on your way to the airport, you have no control over the traffic on the way, possible accidents that might slow down the traffic, cancellation of your flight due to bad weather, etc. So whether you worry and make yourself miserable or listen to music and relax on your way to the airport, the results will be identical. So why make yourself miserable when you are free to relax and be cheerful?

Michel de Montaigne, the French philosopher who lived 500 years ago during the French Renaissance, observed: "My life has been filled with terrible misfortune; most of which never happened." There are research studies to support Michel de Montaigne's observation. In one study quoted by Robert Leahy in his book *Worry Cure*[55], only 15% of what people worry about materialized and even here, in 12% of cases, people coped with the worried outcome better than they had anticipated. This means, if we worry about 100 things, only 3 things we worried about will happen in the way we anticipated. Even among those who have no Stoic training, 97% of worries are for nothing. In the remaining 3% of cases, worrying would not have solved anything anyway. If you had some Stoic training, you would have even less to worry about.

Even though there is evidence to show that most of our worries will never come to pass, the Stoic argument against worrying is not based on that. Even if 100% of all our worries materialize the exact way we anticipated, the Stoic would argue, we still could not change the outcome of a single event by worrying about it. Therefore worrying about what might happen in the future is irrational and it is "against nature," and it does not lead us to freedom. Because we don't have any control over the way things unfold, it is an indifferent. As a result, no purpose is served by worrying. That is Stoic reasoning.

Hedonic treadmill

I read this story somewhere.

A normal guy, despairing of problems he faced in his daily life cried out, "Please God, let these problems go away. Get me out of this miserable life and let me have what I want so I can be happy." God obliged, and the man was sent to heaven. Heaven was wonderful. Whatever he wanted materialized. Hungry? Here was an excellent meal prepared by outstanding chefs. Want to relax? Here's a comfortable place. Want companions? Here were the most interesting and beautiful people you can find anywhere. Want to stroll? Sure enough, the weather was perfect for a stroll. Want to drive? Here was a late model car. You could drive as fast as you like. There were no speed limits and no traffic jams.

He couldn't have been happier. For a while.

Life then got pretty boring. He got what he wanted. All the time. There was no challenge. There was no change. More time passed. The life without challenge, without problems, without anything for him to do except wish for things became excruciatingly painful. He couldn't bear it anymore.

He cried out to God for the second time, "Anything is better than this. Please get me out of here."

God asked, "Anything?"

The man said: "Yes, anything, nothing can be as bad as this."

The man woke up and found himself where he was before he went to heaven. He realized that anything in life was workable, and there was no need to despair.

We get used to anything in our life. Those who do not have a million dollars believe that they would be happy if they did. But the fact is, millionaires are no happier than others. We get used to whatever we have and then crave more. (Or as our protagonist in the story, we crave to be back to where we were. We look back lovingly to the "good old days".)

We believe something will make us happy. Once we get it, we think *something else* will make us happy. When we get that something else, we crave something else again. Whenever we get what we want, we are happy – for a while. Then we go back to our initial level of happiness. This is called the hedonic treadmill.

Sometimes we are not so much anxious about the future as postponing living today in the hope that we will have a better tomorrow. This is the same mistake as worrying about the future. We assume that we know what will happen tomorrow. The fact is that we don't. It is not within our power to know for sure. So whether we worry about a dreaded future or postpone living now because of a rosy future, the result is the same. We give up the freedom to act and be happy now.

Worrying about a dreaded future or hoping for a better one can become a habit. Once it becomes a habit, no matter what happens in the present we continue to dread what might happen in the future or start hoping for even better things. Meanwhile, we miss what happens in the present, no matter how good it is.

And then one day we look back and reminisce about the "good old days" we completely missed. Remember what George Burns said when he was in his nineties? He exclaimed, "Oh to be seventy again!"

The good old days are now. Enjoy what is in front of you now. You are free today. No one can take it away from you.

As Seneca said, "The greatest obstacle to living a full life is having expectations, delaying gratification based on what might happen tomorrow which squanders today."[56]

Appreciating what you have now

Anxieties about the future arise because we believe there is a better place than where we are now. Will we arrive there or not? What if we lost even what we have now? Will things go all right in the future? In being anxious, we forget to enjoy the great things we have now or get used to what we have.

What would we do if we lost things that are dear to us? When we say goodbye to someone, we are not sure if we will ever see them again. Many people, when they hear that their dear ones have passed on, immediately regret not having told them that they loved them and treasured them.

Since whether a person lives or dies is not under our control, it is an "indifferent." Knowing this, we should enjoy the other person's company as long as it lasts but be prepared to give it back because everything is on loan to us. But the Stoics also knew that when we suddenly face such a loss, we are unlikely to react differently than the way we have been conditioned to react all our lives. Even if we do know that what happened is an indifferent, we may be so overcome with grief that we may not be able to apply it to the current situation.

There is a way to enjoy what you have now without anxiety. To do this, you should not always be anxious about a better future but realize the wonderful things you have right now. To make it easier for us to do this, Stoics suggest the regular use of a technique known as "premeditatio malorem." (The term "Negative Visualization" is also used in many blog posts and books to describe this technique.)

THE BIG IDEA 5
We can never lose anything because we don't really own anything

Keep this in mind always: Everything good in our life is given to us. "So why not enjoy this feast and pageant while it is given to you to do so; then when you are ushered out, go with thanks and reverence for what you were privileged for a time to see and hear." (Epictetus[57])

Suggestions for practicing the big idea

Even when we know the future is unpredictable and anything can be taken away from us, for most of us it difficult to remember when something that we think of as "bad" – such as losing our spouse or not getting that promotion – happens to us. It is important to constantly remember that everything is impermanent and uncertain by using the Premeditatio Malorum (Negative Visualization) technique.

Premeditatio Malorum technique (Negative visualization)

Every time you deal with anyone who is dear to you – your parents, your children, your spouse, your friend or your pet – remember that he or she is on loan to you. Remind yourself that you may not see this person ever again. This is literally true. No one can guarantee that you will see anyone again. Make this reminder become a part of your thinking. If something untoward should happen in the future, you will be grateful for the gift that was given to you for all these years and be able to celebrate that person. You would also develop an intense appreciation of the precious person in front of you.

Stoics offered this technique as a means of eliminating a painful reaction to losing people who are dear to us by reminding ourselves that losses are in line with the natural order of things. Seneca used this technique to avoid feeling disappointed in any situation.

There is an unintended (by the Stoics) positive consequence to this technique. When you part with anyone dear to you, suppose you remember that this might be the last time you see them. How would you react? You would probably have an intense appreciation for their presence in your life. You would probably tell them all the nice things you thought about them but did not say. You would have gratitude for the things you have in life. It will help us avoid the trap that Joni Mitchell sang about, "Don't it always seem to go that you don't know what you've got 'til it's gone."

The practice of this *premeditatio malorum* technique will thus increase an appreciation of what we have and acceptance with gratitude when we no longer have the ones we love. It also reminds us not to treat the good things casually, believing that they will always be around. They may not. So let us appreciate what is in front of us and enjoy all the preferred indifferents we are given.

For a complete description of this technique see chapter 14, Stoics and Mental Fitness

CHAPTER 8

Be Free to Enjoy the Festival of life

So why not enjoy the feast and the pageant while it is given to you to do so?

Epictetus

Harlan Ellison is said to have written this wonderful story sitting in the window of a Santa Monica area science fiction bookstore.[58]

The pleasure planet

An ordinary middle-aged person, living a painful and boring life, tries to escape from his terrible life by committing suicide. He then wakes up on a bleak planet inhabited by terrible crab-like beings. He remembers that he had lived on this planet before he lived on Earth and was destined to return to this planet.

He despairs and asks what crime he had committed that he had to endure such a terrible life. He is told that he committed no crime. He had led such an exemplary life on the alien planet that his reward was to spend a lifetime on the pleasure planet called Earth.

Earth, the pleasure planet? Yes! "He remembered the rain and the sleep, and the feel of beach sand beneath his feet, and the ocean rolling in to whisper its eternal song, and on just such nights as those he despised on Earth, he slept and dreamt good dreams… of life on the pleasure planet."[59]

There is so much that life has to offer. But we concentrate on what we lack and fail to notice the wonderful things that surround us on this "pleasure planet," as the protagonist of the above story realizes. We should fully enjoy what life offers us: nature, children's smiles, friendships, exquisite food, fine clothes, etc. We have so many good things around us, we get used to them and don't notice them anymore. Even the seemingly humdrum life of the protagonist of the above story had so many hidden pleasures: "The rain and the sleep, and the feel of beach sand beneath his feet, and the ocean rolling in to whisper its eternal song."

Stoics advise us to feel the joy of life as it presents itself. Happiness comes from the pursuit of the good life rather than the other way around. Because Stoics considered pleasures as indifferents, they didn't actively pursue them but were always ready to enjoy what was in front of them: the feast and the pageant offered to us in the festival of life. Seneca advises his friend,

"Above all, my friend Lucilius, make this your business: learn how to feel joy." [60]

Learn to feel the joy

Stoics were fully aware that things that give us pleasure such as food, music, travel, friends, and family are not under our total control. We may not always have access to good food or music. Our friends may move to a different city. Our family members may die. We may not have the money or the time to travel to far-off places. Because they are not under our total control, they are indifferents, not needed for our freedom. Yet here we are in the festival of life. Many things we consider "good" are right in front of us. Do we let such things pass us by?

No, say the Stoics. Enjoy what is in front of you if it is a preferred indifferent. How would you know if it is a preferred indifferent? Compare smoking with a pleasant meal. Smoking, even though pleasurable, will likely lead to addiction and impaired health. It is a dispreferred indifferent. A pleasant meal can be pleasurable but is unlikely to cause any short-term or long-term damage (unless one indulges in excessive eating). It has few negative consequences. So it is a preferred indifferent. In fact, anything that you like that does not have negative consequences to you or to others is a preferred indifferent.

So as you go through life, feel free to enjoy the preferred indifferents which are many: friends, family, the sunrise, the sunset, the seasons, the wonders of the world, travel. In fact, in

the modern world, we have access to an endless variety of preferred indifferents. Even if you face your death, there is no reason not to enjoy what is in front of you. Remember what
Epictetus said: "I have to die? If it is now, then I will die now; if
later, then I will have my lunch now, since the hour for lunch
has arrived – and dying I will tend to later." Even impending
death is no hindrance to enjoying what is in front of you. Do not
worry about what others think. Enjoy with no guilt.

Seneca advised, "We should take walks outside so the mind
can be strengthened and refreshed by being outdoors as we
breathe the fresh air. Sometimes it will get new vigor from a trip
by carriage and a change of place, along with festive company
and generous drinking."[61] While some Stoics might disagree
with the "generous drinking" part, his sentiments are very much
in line with Stoic joy.

Don't go after happiness, let happiness find you

Advice like that given by Seneca could have been given by a
non-Stoic or even by someone who does not believe in Stoic
principles. The difference between Stoic joy and joy as we understand it is this: a Stoic would continue to look for living well
wherever he is, even if what he enjoys now is taken away from
him. For Stoics, there is a difference between transient pleasures and a consistent sense of well-being. To get pleasure, we
can have a drink or two every evening. We can have a gourmet

meal. We can watch a show. All these things are pleasurable, and pleasurable things provide a sense of well-being.

However, using pleasure alone as the basis for well-being has a downside to it. We get used to these pleasures. Once we get used to these pleasures, we want a more intense form of the same thing or something else. For example, if you have a drink every evening in a bar, after a while the drink becomes a necessity and does not evoke the same degree of pleasure as before. You may want a second drink to feel as good as you did with one drink a few months before. If you derive pleasure by going shopping every week, after a while that becomes a necessity and, to derive the same enjoyment, you may have to spend more on shopping.

If you generally go to McDonalds and sometimes you get to go to an expensive restaurant, you may derive a great deal of pleasure from the more upscale restaurant. But if you start going to an expensive restaurant as frequently as you had been going to McDonalds, you are likely to get used to the expensive restaurant and not feel as good as you did about it the first few times. It may no longer evoke the same sense of well-being as it did earlier. People who have made money crave even more. What was a want becomes a need, once we get used to it. Psychologists call this hedonistic adaptation.

Even more to the point, the major downside to pursuing pleasure directly is that it generally involves external things that are not under our control. These pleasures can be taken away from you. You may not be able to afford to go to an expensive restaurant often, your health conditions may no longer allow you to drink alcohol, and you may not be affluent enough to afford expensive shopping trips. If you derive pleasure through travel, you may develop health conditions which may prevent you from traveling even if you can afford it.

For these reasons, Stoics didn't go after pleasures as primary sources of well-being. They did not pursue external things to derive happiness directly. Rather, they believed that we need to lead a virtuous life, a life that is in conformity with nature, according to rationality or logic. A virtuous life in Stoicism is a life of wisdom, justice, courage, and self-discipline. Such a life is a rational life. Therefore it is the good life which includes a sense of well-being, freedom, and happiness. Freedom is a by-product of the good life.

Don't go after happiness but seek the good life. When you seek the good life by acting according to nature, freedom finds you as much as you find freedom.

Find joy under all conditions

The way of Stoic joy is this. Enjoy and appreciate whatever is in front of you. If it is snatched from you, don't feel miserable. Look around and see what else can bring you well-being now. If you are invited to a party, enjoy the company of friends and the good food offered to you. If you are not invited, don't complain. Instead, eat a nourishing meal, enjoy the company of those at home. If you cannot even afford a nourishing meal, chew on a slice of bread and enjoy some fresh air. Always using what is under your control to bring you joy is the Stoic way.

Seneca said, "True happiness is to enjoy the present, without anxious dependence upon the future, not to amuse ourselves with either hopes or fears but to rest satisfied with what we have, which is sufficient, for he that is so wants nothing. The greatest blessings of mankind are within us and within our reach. A wise man is content with his lot, whatever it may be, without wishing for what he has not." [62]

American science fiction writer and professor, Isaac Asimov, put it this way: "Maybe happiness is this: not feeling you should be elsewhere, doing something else, being someone else."

Marcus Aurelius would have approved of Asimov. Marcus said, "If you apply yourself to living only that which you are living – in other words the present – then you can live the rest of your life until your death in peace, benevolence, and serenity." [63]

So enjoy the festival of life as it is now. If something is taken away from you, don't concern yourself with what you don't have. Enjoy what you have left. Remember what Agrippinus said when he learned he was exiled? "Let's go to Aricia and have lunch there!"

Avoid regrets

A Stoic does not regret what happened in the past or what she had once because it is already gone. Instead, she enjoys whatever is in front of her and under her control with great joy. An ideal Stoic gives herself no cause to regret in the future because she enjoys whatever life has to offer at the moment.

Even when you feel everything is going wrong, still you have something: your life. As Carlos Castaneda observed, "Whenever you feel... that everything is going wrong, and you're about to be annihilated, turn to your death and ask if that is so. Your death will tell you that you're wrong; that nothing really matters outside its touch. Your death will tell you, "I haven't touched you yet." [64] As long as you have this thing called life, and as long as you can clearly distinguish what is under your control and what is not, you are free to enjoy the festival of life. Look at all the preferred indifferents in your life right now. It is for us to enjoy what is in front of us.

THE BIG IDEA 6
Life is a festival. Enjoy it now.

"True happiness is... to enjoy the present, without anxious dependence upon the future." (Seneca[65])

We constantly crave things we don't have. But when we do get them, we crave more things. While we live life this way, we miss the festival of life. The festival of life is on now right where you are. Feel free to enjoy it.

Suggestions for practicing the big idea

Enjoying the festival of life requires us to let go of our ingrained habits of anxiety. So, to enjoy life, we need constant reminders to look at life differently. For this purpose, we have three Stoic techniques: the Anticipatory Prep (Morning Mediation), the

Passion Counter, and the Course Correction (End-of-the-day Meditation).

While you can sit in a meditative posture and do the morning and evening meditations, if you are not inclined to do that, you can do them in your bed as you wake up in the morning and at night, again in your bed, before going to sleep. One great thing about Stoicism is that, while it emphasizes practice, it does not require that you make any specific time investment.

---

1. The Anticipatory Prep technique (Morning meditation)

You may feel you are unable to enjoy the festival of life because things don't go the way you expect. To prepare yourself for this, you can start the day anticipating the possible ways in which your day can go wrong and prepare yourself for them. Use this technique to forestall negatively reacting to others when they behave in a way that might annoy you. It is also a very pleasant way to start the day.

When you awake in the morning, you can continue to lie in bed for a while. Let your attention focus on these thoughts.

Gratitude. What have you learned from others over the years? Who taught you the many things you know now? Your parents, your teachers, your friends, your spouse. As they come to your mind one by one, thank them silently for making you who you are. Did anyone make your life a little better yesterday?

The shopkeeper who smiled at you while serving? The super-market checkout clerk who patiently bagged all your groceries? Let them come to mind. Silently thank them.

Preparation. As you continue relaxing in bed, mentally pre-pare yourself to face the world. Say to yourself, "Today I will meet with people who are meddling, unthankful, rude, disloyal, and selfish. People who behave this way don't know the differ-ence between what is good and evil. But, because I know the difference, I will not be affected by their behavior. Neither will I be angry or be irritated because I'd rather cooperate than fight with others." Repeat to yourself: "Today I will control only what is under my control. I will not worry about things not in my control." Later in the day, whenever you face any unpleasant encounter, recall these words.

Cheerfulness. You are now ready to face the world. Get up cheerfully. If you are still reluctant to get up, continue on your meditation for a while and say to yourself, "I am here to do the work of a human being. Why should I feel I am not up to it and lie in bed? Like every being that does the work assigned to it, I can do the work of a human being too." Now get up cheerfully.

2. The Passion Counter technique (through the day)

Our enjoyment of the festival of life is often ruined by a burst of negative emotions such as anger and fear. When you believe you are susceptible to some specific negative emotion such as anger, to loosen its grip, you can use the Passion Counter tech-nique throughout the day.

- Carry a pocket counter (which you can probably buy in a dollar store) with you all day. If you don't want to use a counter, carry a small notebook.

- Throughout the day, whenever you feel anger coming on, click the counter (or tally it in your notebook).

- Do it while it happens or immediately afterward. Don't leave it to later, because we tend to forget unless we record it right away.

- Just before going to sleep (or earlier if you prefer) gently review how many times your passion got the better of you.

When you keep using this technique without trying to change anything, you will notice the undesired behavior becoming less and less frequent. As Epictetus put it

> *Vice begins to weaken from day one, until it is wiped out altogether. "I didn't lose my temper this day, or the next, and not for two, then three months in." If you can say that, you're now in excellent health, believe me.*[66]

3. The Course Correction technique (End-of-day meditation)

One reason why we don't enjoy the festival of life is that we keep repeating the same unproductive behavior. We tend to forget what is under our control and what is not. The Course Correction technique makes us take note of our behavior. This, along with the Anticipatory Prep technique, can be used daily to increase our enjoyment of the festival of life.

1. As you are about to sleep (or earlier if you prefer), review the events of the day.
2. What threatened your freedom? Did you experience feelings of anger, resentment, fear, and frustration? When?
3. Understand how violating the principle of trying to control what is not under your control caused these negative feelings and deprived you of your freedom.
4. How would you handle it using Stoic principles of freedom?
5. Imagine yourself handling it that way if a similar situation arose in the future. If you feel like it, repeat the gratitude part of the morning meditation before going to bed.

Seneca explains this well:

> Proceed with steady step, and if you would have all things under your control, put yourself under the control of reason; if reason becomes your ruler, you will become ruler over many. You will learn from her what you should undertake, and how it should be done; you will not blunder into things... It is disgraceful, instead of proceeding ahead, to be carried along, and then suddenly, amid the whirlpool of events, to ask in a dazed way: "How did I get into this condition?"[67]

For a complete description of these three techniques see chapter 14, Stoics and Mental Fitness.

PART III

REVIEW AND EXPLORE

Let's review and consolidate what we have
discussed thus far

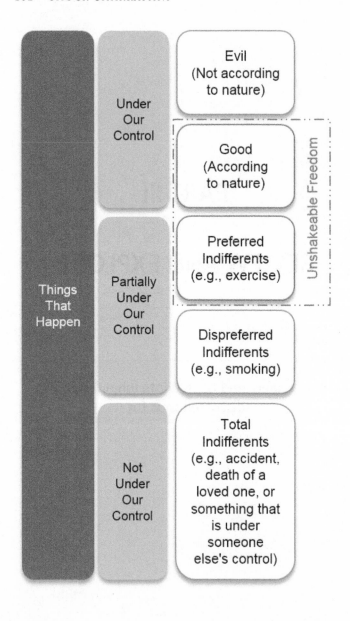

CHAPTER 9

The Stoic
Model of Freedom

In this and the next part of the book, we will not introduce any new ideas. Instead, we will review and consolidate what we have discussed thus far, adding some supporting material.

The Stoic model of freedom is different from the way most of us seek freedom. The Stoic model reverses the way we seek freedom, happiness, and serenity.

The Stoic model vs. conventional models

The way most people seek freedom is to do things that they think will lead them to freedom. If they succeed, they are happy. If they fail, they feel miserable. Since we can never be sure whether we will succeed or not before the results of our actions are known, we may also feel stressed about the possibility of failing. No one can *guarantee* that we would succeed in anything in our life. There are too many unknowns outside our control.

Conventional Model

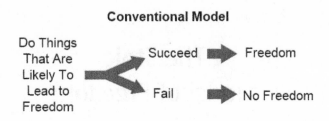

Stoics saw things differently. They did not go after freedom directly. Instead, they held that we would achieve the good life or eudemonia by living a "virtuous" life consistent with reason. Freedom is a by-product of the good life, a result of living according to reason.

Stoic Model

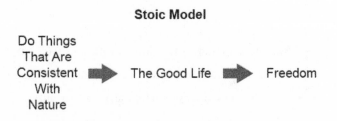

The Stoic model guarantees freedom because it confines itself to what is under our control.

Achieving freedom

When you go through life, you have to clearly distinguish what is within your power and what is not. Your opinions, desires, and aversions, your actions are completely within your power. Nothing else is.

When you act according to nature, your acts are "good" and they contribute to your freedom and happiness. When you act against nature, your acts are "evil" because they do not contribute to your freedom and happiness. The good life is attained by acting rationally which by definition leads to freedom.

Things that are not completely within your power are "indifferents," they are not needed for your freedom. Indifferents that are partially in your power, if they can be considered desirable (such as your health) are preferred indifferents.

As long as you confine your actions to (a) those that are in your control and according to nature; and (b) those that are only partially in your control but still according to nature, you will achieve total freedom. But you should be fully aware that the things that are under your partial control are on indefinite loan to you and can be taken away from you at any time.

Your actions need to be virtuous. Stoic "virtue" is somewhat different from what we mean by virtue when we use the word these days. For the Stoics, virtue means "excelling" or "flourishing" and it involves developing these four qualities: *wisdom* (resourcefulness and discretion), *justice* (honesty), *courage*, and *self-discipline*. A person who lives rationally would be wise, just, courageous, and self-disciplined. To make it even simpler, we can consider a virtuous action as one that is "according to nature." What is according to nature is what is in line with reason.

Similarly, the Stoics divided vice into *foolishness, injustice, cowardice, intemperance,* and *the rest.* Note that the Stoic conception of vice (like their conception of virtue) has more to do with "not acting according to nature" or acting non-rationally and does not relate to any religious or moral connotation.

This chart that follows summarizes the Stoic model. As long as we confine our actions to the second and third boxes as shown, we will be free of all hindrances. *The only and important caveat is that, while are free to enjoy the preferred indifferents, they are simply a bonus, and we should be prepared to give them up with no notice.* In fact, we should always be conscious of their impermanence.

Things That Happen

Under Our Control
- Evil (Not according to nature)
- Good (According to nature)

Partially Under Our Control
- Preferred Indifferents (e.g., exercise)
- Dispreferred Indifferents (e.g., smoking)

Not Under Our Control
- Total Indifferents (e.g., accident, death of a loved one, or something that is under someone else's control)

Unshakeable Freedom

Summary of stoic premises

Basic Ideas

1. Some things in our life are under our complete control, and others are not. Things under our complete control are what we believe, what we desire or hate, and what we move toward or avoid. Other things are not in our complete control.

2. We can be free and happy by controlling only what is in our total control.

3. We should aim for a rational life which can also be termed as "life according to nature" or a "virtuous life." For the Stoics, virtue means *wisdom* (resourcefulness and discretion), *justice* (honesty), *courage*, and *moderation*. A person who lives rationally would be wise, just, courageous, and moderate.

4. We should avoid a life that is not according to reason, a life that includes vices: *foolishness, injustice, cowardice, intemperance,* and *the rest*.

5. Whatever is not under our total control is not necessary for our freedom. They are indifferents.

6. If things are under our partial control, we can pursue them if they are desirable indifferents, as long as we remember that they are not under our control.

7. We should enjoy whatever life offers us but shouldn't chase after things.

Stoic big ideas used in this book

This book is built on the core Stoic idea that some things in our life are under our control and others are not. It is possible to achieve total freedom by just concentrating on what we can control. In addition, the book is based on six big ideas derived from the core Stoic idea:

Big idea 1. Problems are only problems if you believe they are.

"Put away the belief 'I've been wronged,' and with it will go the feeling. Reject your sense of injury and the injury itself disappears." (Marcus Aurelius)

Big idea 2. Leave your past behind.

"All the happiness you are seeking by such long, roundabout ways, you can have it all right now... if you leave all the past behind you." (Marcus Aurelius)

Big idea 3. Don't let the indifferents rob your freedom.

Avoid having opinions on things that happen every day. You are not in charge of other people's behavior; they will act as they please.

Big idea 4. Where there is fear, freedom is not.

"One way to guarantee freedom it to be ready to die." (Epictetus) We forego freedom when we are afraid. It leads us to do things that are not in line with the good life. Because a Stoic values mental freedom above physical freedom, he is not afraid.

Big idea 5. You can never lose anything because you don't own anything.

Keep this in mind always: everything good in our life is given to us. "So why not enjoy this feast and pageant while it is given to you to do so; then when you are ushered out, go with thanks and reverence for what you were privileged for a time to see and hear." (Epictetus)

Big idea 6. Life is a festival. Enjoy it now.

"True happiness is… to enjoy the present, without anxious dependence upon the future." (Seneca[68])

Stoic joy

Enjoy what life has to offer, but don't go after pleasures for their own sake. Even if you expect to die tomorrow, enjoy each meal today. Life offers a lot of preferred indifferents. Use them to generate joy but be willing to let them go when the time comes.

Stoic fearlessness

William Shakespeare, who is said to have had some Stoic influence, wrote, "A coward dies a thousand times before his death, but the valiant taste of death but once. It seems to me most strange that men should fear, seeing that death, a necessary end, will come when it will come." This is precisely the Stoic view. To the Stoic, death is a natural part of life, and there's no reason to be fearful about it. It can come only once. A Stoic is not afraid to die. She knows it is inevitable. If she has to die now, so be it. But until death comes, a Stoic will act as though everything is the way it should be, because it is. Whatever you face is what nature has intended, so for a person living according to nature, there is nothing to fear.

Stoics and passions

Stoics, although rational, are not passionless. They mindfully distinguish what really contributes to their freedom from what does not — virtue versus vice. This uncompromising and consistent understanding keeps the ups and downs out of their lives. They believe whatever happens to them is what nature intended and therefore they are fearless. Their serenity and freedom come from this fearlessness and not from lack of passion.

The virtuous person is not passionless in the sense of being unfeeling like a statue. Rather, he mindfully distinguishes what makes a difference to his happiness from what does not — virtue versus vice. This firm and consistent understanding keeps the ups and downs of his life from spinning into the psychic disturbances or "pathologies" the Stoics understood passions to be.

In our current usage, "passions" as used by Stoics would refer to negative emotions such as anger, excessive greed, envy, etc., that overpower our reason and lead us to 'vices" such as foolishness, injustice, cowardice, and intemperance.

Stoic mind-training techniques

The Stoics were masters of thought experiments. They mention their thought experiments in their writing. These can be used as training techniques. We have discussed these techniques throughout the book. I have gathered these techniques and present them in the last chapter of this book for convenient access.

CHAPTER 10

Where did Stoicism Come From?

Around fifth century BCE, a number of philosophers who were not connected to each other by geography, language, or religion started thinking about the best way to live: Buddha in India, Confucius and Lao-Tzu in China, and Diogenes of Sinope in Greece. We have no reason to believe that they knew of each other. Here we will concern ourselves with Greek/Roman philosophy, Stoicism in particular. Most of us have heard of Cynicism, Epicureanism, and Stoicism. The current dictionary meanings of these terms are far removed from what they meant two thousand years ago when these philosophies flourished.

Greek philosophers believed that the goal of philosophy is *eudemonia*. Eudemonia is what we would call the good life or flourishing. While there was widespread agreement among Greek philosophers that eudemonia was the desired end result, they differed on how they thought one could achieve it. Such differences led to the establishment of different schools of Greek philosophy such as Peripateticism, Cynicism, Epicurean-ism, and Stoicism.

The forerunner of Stoicism was Cynicism, led by Diogenes. Cynicism can be seen as a more ascetic form of Stoicism. Cynics believed essentially what the Stoics believed: things under our control are enough to make us free. Cynics despised what was not under control. They lived an ascetic life, and Diogenes of Sinope (412 or 404 BCE - 323 BCE) was a major practitioner of this movement. Diogenes, for example, wore a coarse garment, lived in a barrel, and begged for food.

Zeno of Citium (334 – 262 BCE) founded Stoicism. He based his philosophy on the moral ideas developed by Diogenes. Stoicism emphasized goodness and peace of mind gained through living a life of virtue in accordance with nature. Stoi-cism, in general, advocated a gentler version of Cynicism: do not turn away from things not under your complete control. In-stead, enjoy them if they are good for you but be prepared to give them back at short notice.

Early Stoa. Early Stoicism extended between about 300 BCE and 175 BCE. Its leaders in this period included Zeno, Cle-anthes, Chrysippus, Diogenes of Babylon, and Antipater of Tar-sus.

Middle Stoa. Middle Stoicism (between 150 BCE to 50 BCE) was led by Panaetius and Posidonius. During this period, Cicero wrote a book re-expressing Stoic arguments.

Late Stoa. Late Stoicism flourished in Rome. While little exists of the writings of early and middle Stoa, this is not the case with late Stoa. Late Stoa flourished for about 150 years starting about the time of Christ. Exponents of late Stoa included Musonius Rufus, Seneca the Younger, Epictetus, and Marcus Aurelius. The Stoics held Socrates in high esteem. Socrates may well be the honorary godfather of Stoicism.

Who were the Stoics? They were philosophers who tried to answer the question "How to live well?" They came up with some answers which were tested under some of the most harrowing human conditions and were found to hold.

CHAPTER 11

Freedom That Can't Be Taken from You

Life is full of ups and downs.

Everything changes. We are happy for a while and then we are not. We get married, and we get divorced. We are born, and we die. We acquire friends, and they move away. We get jobs, and we lose them. Seasons change. Investments grow, and investments collapse. We are young, and then we are no longer young. What we thought was permanent is no longer permanent. The world around us is constantly changing.

We have minimal control over other people, things, or events. We feel unfree because people don't behave the way we expect or would like them to, events don't turn out the way we want them to, and we can't always get what we want. Even if people behave today the way we expect them to, even if we have all the things we desire, and even if everything happened according to our wishes, things may all change tomorrow, next month, or next year. What then?

Clearly, if we leave our freedom to things that are outside of us – things, people, and events – we cannot really be free. No emperor, no billionaire, no scientist has ever been able to control the world around them totally. But many people have lived a free life. It follows then freedom cannot and should not depend on people around you changing, events happening according to your liking, and your having to acquire certain things in life.

To apply the Stoic philosophy, you need to follow no dogma, no religion, no mystic principle, and no political party. It is a philosophy that is based on thinking rationally about our freedom and taking the path that is open to us all. While the ancient Stoics taught Stoicism as an entire system including ethics, physics, and logic, they were fully aware that people don't have to buy into the entire Stoic system to benefit from it. As a matter of fact, Cleanthes actually said that he could teach peace of mind to anyone, including those who did not believe in Stoicism. The core idea of Stoicism is that we can achieve freedom solely by controlling what is fully under our control. We saw example after example of real people living in the modern world practicing this philosophy to set themselves free.

You may have your wealth, your health, your loved ones, and your prized possessions. But all of these you can lose or have taken away from you. It is not that unusual for a rich person to lose her wealth, and for a healthy person to suddenly be afflicted by Parkinson's disease or cancer. Our loved ones may die, and our possessions can be stolen. But the freedom offered by the Stoics cannot be taken away from us.

Such freedom cannot be achieved without constant practice and vigilance. Stoic mind training techniques, if practiced regularly, will break the shackles that bind you.

It is a path that is less traveled but leads you to unshakable freedom. That is the way of the Stoics.

PART IV

WORK OUT
IN THE STOIC GYM

Do freedom workouts in the Stoic gym

CHAPTER 12

Unshakable Freedom: Reality or Fantasy?

Unshakable freedom was what the Stoics promised. You might be still skeptical. Is it possible to achieve it or is it chasing a fantasy? Of the possibly hundreds of thousands of people who practice some form of Stoicism today, how many actually achieve unshakable freedom?

From the lives of philosophers, it is possible to deduce that such freedom is possible. Socrates refused to flee when given the opportunity to do so and faced his death cheerfully. Helvidius faced the Emperor to let him know that if the Emperor killed him, he (Helvidius) would die without flinching. Epictetus kept his zest for life intact when he was a slave, when his leg was broken, and when he was banished. He never thought he was unfree.

Seneca was experiencing a luxurious life when he was charged with adultery with Julia Livilla, sister of Emperor Caligula in 41 CE and exiled to Corsica. His child had died, and he had lost his father and siblings as well as money, possessions, and his influential position. A good time to understand the effectiveness of Stoic principles. Can they work under such extreme conditions? We know because, around this time, Seneca wrote a letter to his mother and this is what he had to say: "To assure you... I can't even be made wretched. All those things that [nature] has bestowed upon me – money, public office, and influence – I relegated to a place whence she can claim them back without bothering me... I have kept a wide gap between them and me, with the result she has taken them away, not torn them away." His exile was just a 'change of place' and it did not bring him feelings of disgrace.

Unshakable freedom is also exhibited by James Stockdale, Rhonda Cornum, Warren Zevon, Mahatma Gandhi, Malala Yousafzai, Nelson Mandela, and many others in modern times.

But still, of the many who practice, how many achieve unshakable freedom? To answer this question, we need to understand the context in which Stoicism was developed. It was developed at a time when people could keep slaves and deprive them of all freedom. People could break a slave's leg to pass the time. Gladiators could be forced to fight to the death for the entertainment of onlookers. A tyrant or a mad ruler like Nero could kill anyone (even if she was his mother) or banish anyone, just because he felt so inclined. Stoicism was an antidote to the unpredictable life that confronted them. People needed a philosophy that would protect them no matter what happened to them. To achieve total freedom from the unpredictable dangers they constantly faced, they practiced Stoicism seriously.

If you are free enough and literate enough to read this, then the chances are that you are not a slave, you will not be forced to fight unto death, probably no one is going to throw you in jail arbitrarily, and you can't be banished from your country. I would also assume that you are not reading this book to prepare to be free in case you are captured by a terrorist and beheaded. Most likely you would like to be free of past worries, free of the day-to-day problems of living, free of anxieties about the future, free of grief when something bad happens, and perhaps even be prepared to a certain extent to face imprisonment or danger to your person. If that were the case, the chances are that you would like to spend some time practicing Stoicism, but may not want to make it your only focus in life.

Like most things in life, our practice follows the Pareto principle. If we want a noticeable improvement in the quality of our life, consciously practicing Stoic principles even a few minutes a day on a consistent basis will result in an increased sense of freedom, happiness, and serenity. It will help you cope with unexpected events. For all practical purposes, you will be free. However, unshakable freedom is available to us if we are willing to diligently practice Stoic techniques for achieving it.

For me, unshakable freedom is freedom from daily anxieties and worries and keeping my cool under conditions that would have disturbed the pre-Stoic me, so that I can enjoy the festival of life. I believe I am on my way to achieving this and, with consistent practice and study, anyone can do this. It does not require a lot of time investment, just the commitment to remind ourselves constantly what is under our control and what is not. Regularly working out in the Stoic Gym will definitely help.

CHAPTER 13

Freedom and Physical Fitness

Adapt to cold, heat, thirst, hunger, plain food, a hard bed, abstinence from pleasure and endurance of strenuous labor.

Musonius Rufus

P hysical fitness enables us to carry on our daily activities with ease, freeing us to pursue what is important in life. Ancient philosophers, therefore, kept themselves physically fit. Plato (whose name means "broadshouldered") was a renowned wrestler. Socrates was regarded as the toughest soldier in the Athenian army.

Stoics did not neglect their bodies. There is evidence that many Stoic philosophers were physically robust. Chrysippus was a long distance runner and died laughing at the age of 73 during the 143rd Olympiad[69]. Cleanthes was a boxer. Marcus Aurelius was a warrior and actually expressed thanks to the gods for giving him the body that could withstand so much stress. Epictetus' body was strong enough to endure physical disability, slavery, and banishment. The teacher of Epictetus, Musonius Rufus, advised his students to exercise both mind and body.

Yet, to the Stoic, the body is not important. The body is vulnerable to attacks, illnesses, accidents, and even death. It is not under our control. Because the body is an indifferent, no matter what happens to it, we can still be free. A good body supports mental freedom but is not needed for it. So why did the Stoics, along with other ancient philosophers, cultivate their body? The simple reason is that health is partially under our control, and it is a preferred indifferent.

So if you are a Stoic, you would look after your body through proper nutrition and exercise, so your body serves you well. However, you would not be obsessed with it because it is not under your control and it is not essential for your freedom.

What then is essential for your freedom? A mind that is in tune with nature. So, while the Stoics gave no specific advice on how to cultivate the body, they left us with a wide range of exercises designed to cultivate a mind that is totally free.

CHAPTER 14

Freedom and
Mental Fitness

*How could anyone gain self-control, if he only knew theoretically
that one should resist pleasure, but never practiced resisting it?*

Musonius Rufus

A mind that is in tune with nature does not happen by accident. It is one thing to know what would make us free, but it is quite another to be able to use what we know when we need to use it. A physics professor could explain in great detail how a tightrope walker walks the rope. This doesn't mean the professor would be able to do it himself. It is so with any skill. Knowledge is important, but practice is more important.

The importance of practice

One cannot achieve freedom by reading books or listening to lectures. No matter how well you understand the principles, unless you practice them regularly, you won't be able to use them when you need them. When we are in the grip of emotions, when we have to decide quickly, the chances are that our earlier conditioning will assert itself in a way inconsistent with our freedom. Our past conditioning will prove to be much stronger than the recent insights we may have acquired. "How could anyone gain self-control," asks the Stoic philosopher Rufus, "if he only knew theoretically that one should resist pleasure, but never practiced resisting it?"

Seneca also emphasizes the importance of regular practice with these words: "The mind should be exercised both day and night because it is nourished by moderate labor. And this form of exercise need not be hampered by cold or hot weather or even by old age." Routine excuses such as weather and old age are not acceptable.

The only way we can get rid of past conditioning and act in a way that is consistent with our freedom is to put the new insights into consistent action.

The stoic gym

When we start practicing the new insights, we especially need help, like a young person using training wheels before riding a regular bicycle. For this, Stoics have suggested a number of techniques. They didn't call them techniques and did not give them names. However, strewn in their teachings are clues as to how we can train ourselves to use Stoic principles on a day-to-day basis. They would be as useful to a neophyte as to an experienced practitioner of Stoicism.

The Stoics did not create a "Workbook" for practitioners. Instead, in their teaching they suggested (often indirectly) a number of exercises by using the tools they excelled at: logic, thought experiments, use of analogies, and rhetorical questions. I was mostly successful in identifying instances from their writings that can be used in developing exercises. However, occasionally I could not find anything that was directly suitable. In such cases, I created exercises "inspired" by Stoic writings rather than by anything directly suggested by them.

This is the Stoic gym. These are some of the exercises.

The first two exercises are morning and evening meditation. You can sit in a quiet place, close your eyes, and do these meditations for about 10 to 20 minutes. If you prefer not to allocate time specifically for this purpose, you can simply lie in bed. What is really important is not the duration of the meditation or even the posture, but the calmness and clarity with which you do practice.

I have described these training techniques throughout the book. Here, I have collected them in one place, added some clarifications and presented them in a consistent format to make them more useful for practitioners. I have given them names so they can be remembered and recalled quickly when needed.

1. The Anticipatory Prep technique (Morning meditation)

The Anticipatory Prep technique is a form of morning meditation, best done as soon as you wake up. It prepares you for the day ahead.

When to use it

Use this technique every morning and as needed.

What to use it for

Use Anticipatory Prep to forestall negatively reacting to others when they behave in a way that might annoy you. It is also a very pleasant way to start the day.

How does the Anticipatory Preparation technique work?

When you are up in the morning, continue to lie in bed for a while. Think these thoughts:

1. Give gratitude.

Think of all the things and people you should be thankful for. What have you learned from others over the years? Who taught you the many things you know now? Your parents, your teachers, your friends, your spouse? Let them come to your mind one by one. Thank them for making you who you are.

Who made your life a little better yesterday? The barista at the coffee shop who smiled at you while serving? The supermarket checkout clerk who patiently bagged all your groceries? Let them come to mind. Silently thank them.

2. Prepare for the day.

Continue to lie in bed and say to yourself, "Today I will meet with people who are meddling, unthankful, rude, disloyal, and selfish. People who behave this way don't know the difference between good and evil. But, because I know the difference, I will not be affected by their behavior. Neither will I be angry or be irritated because I'd rather cooperate than fight with others."

Repeat to yourself, "Today I will control only what is under my control. I will not worry about things not in my control." Later in the day, whenever you face any unpleasant encounter, recall these words.

3. Get up cheerfully.

Once you have prepared your mind this way, get up cheerfully. If you are still reluctant to get up, continue on your meditation for a while and say to yourself, "I am here to do the work of a human being. Why should I feel I am not up to it and lie in bed? Like every being that does the work assigned to it, I can do the work of a human being too."

In their own words

Giving gratitude.

Marcus Aurelius devotes the first of 12 "books" (chapters) entirely to acknowledging what he received from others. He begins thus: "From grandfather: character and self-control; from father: integrity and manliness," and continues on acknowledging what he learned from 17 different sources.

Preparing for the day.

"Today I shall be meeting with interference, ingratitude, insolence, disloyalty, ill-will, and selfishness – all of them due to the offenders' ignorance of what is good or evil. But for my part… (n)either can I be angry with my brother or fall foul of him. To obstruct each other is against Nature's law – and what is irritation or aversion but a form of obstruction."[70]

Getting up cheerfully.

"In the morning, when you have trouble getting out of bed, tell yourself: "I have to go work like a human being, if I am going to do what I was born for… Or was I created to huddle under the blankets and keep myself warm?"[71]

---

2. The Course Correction technique (End-of-day meditation)

This is a useful technique, used at the end of every day to review how rationally we lived during the day and prepare ourselves better for the following day.

When to use it

Use this technique at the end of every day.

What to use it for

Use the Course Correction technique to identify instances where you have forgotten to apply the principle of concerning yourself with only things under your control, without worrying about things not under your control.

How does the Course Correction technique work?

Just before going to sleep (or earlier if you prefer) go through the events of the day. Particularly pay attention to events that threatened your freedom: feelings like anger, resentment, fear, and frustration.

Examine how violating Stoic principles by trying to control what is not under your control caused these negative feelings and deprived you of your freedom. If you have been using the Passion Counter technique (see next exercise for details of this technique) throughout the day, review the events.

Don't be critical of yourself. Remember also the instances in which you did things that were in line with your freedom. Imagine how you would course-correct using Stoic principles of freedom. Imagine yourself handling it that way if a similar situation arose in the future. If you feel like it, repeat the gratitude part of the morning meditation before going to bed.

In their own words

"Every day, we must call upon our soul to give an account of itself... 'What evils have you cured yourself of today? What vices have you fought? In what sense are you better?' How tranquil, deep, and free it is, when the mind has been praised or warned, and has become the observer and secret judge of its own morals! I make use of this power, and every day I plead my cause before myself... I hide nothing from myself, nor am I indulgent with myself."[72]

3. The Passion Counter technique

Use this technique throughout the day, especially when you believe you are susceptible to some specific negative emotions such as anger.

When to use it

Use it throughout the day.

What to use it for

Use it whenever negative emotions such as anger (or "passion" to use the Stoic language) that you are concerned about arise.

How does the Passion Counter technique work?

1. Carry a pocket counter (which you can probably buy in a dollar store) with you all day. If you don't want to buy a counter, carry a small notebook.

2. Throughout the day, whenever you feel anger coming on, click the counter (or tally it in your notebook).

3. Do it while it happens or immediately afterward. Don't leave it to later, because we tend to forget unless we record it right away.

Just keep a tally. You don't need to judge yourself or struggle to change your behavior. The main idea behind this exercise is to become conscious of the fact that we are often in the grip of negative emotions, and we are mostly unaware of it. Before going to sleep (or earlier if you prefer) simply review the events of the day and remember the count for the day. As you become more and more aware of the grip of negative emotions, they will start losing their hold on you.

In their own words

"At first keep calm and quiet and count... I used to experience negative emotion ["passion"] everyday, then every other day, then every third day and every fourth and so on... the habit first begins to be weakened then eventually is completely destroyed."[73]

---

4. The Pause and Examine technique

When to use it

Use Pause and Examine whenever any situation is about to generate a negative emotion like anger, grief, etc.

What to use it for

Whenever you need to understand the true nature of what is upsetting you, use the Pause and Examine technique. This will guide you to act rationally towards the situation as opposed to emotionally over-reacting.

How does the Pause and Examine technique work?

When you feel a negative emotion, don't get carried away. Take time to examine what appears to be upsetting you. "Appearance, wait for me a while. Let me see who you are, and what you represent. Let me test you." For example, you are angry with someone, and you want to get back at them. You don't immediately act on it but pause for a while to examine your emotion.

Realize that the appearance is telling you a story and painting a rosy picture of acting on negative emotions. For example, your emotions could be telling you that you would be "teaching him a lesson" by angrily shouting at someone, and it is a desirable thing. Do not believe the story.

Instead, examine the event. Is controlling what other people do within your power or is it an indifferent? Clearly, it is an indifferent.

Replace your anger with more positive thoughts that are in line with your freedom and happiness. For example, replace your angry thoughts with thoughts like, "I am unlikely to achieve much by being angry. I cannot control what other people do anyway. I would rather be free than be angry."

In their own words

"Work, therefore to be able to say to every harsh appearance, 'You are but an appearance, and not absolutely the thing you appear to be.' And then examine it by those rules which you have, and first, and chiefly, by this: whether it concerns the things which are in your control or not; and if it concerns anything not in your control, be prepared to say that it is nothing to you."[74]

---

5. The Two Handles technique

When to use it

Use the Two Handles technique whenever you are upset by the actions of other people, especially those you are close to.

What to use it for

The main purpose of the Two Handles technique is to give yourself more than one option, so you choose the one that leads to freedom.

How does the Two Handles technique work?

The Two Handles technique is based on the understanding that there are always two ways to handle any situation. One is compatible with freedom, and the other is not.

- Suppose your friend did something to hurt you.

- The handle, "My friend hurt me" leads to anger and other negative consequences. When we are angry, we are in the clutches of a negative emotion and therefore not free. So this handle cannot be used here.

- The other handle is, "She is my friend and we have shared many past experiences together, we have many things in common, she has done many good things for me in the past, even if she has done now something that I think is wrong." This is better suited for the current situation.

- When we use the second handle, we don't feel hindered by our friend's actions or by our anger. When you are upset with your boss, the handle, "He is a jerk," or, "He doesn't appreciate me," or, "He doesn't know what he is talking about," or, 'He is being unreasonable," is the incorrect handle. The handle, "I am grateful I have this job. Let me see why my boss is asking me to do this. Let me understand this from her perspective," is likely to diffuse anger and likely to lead to a more pleasant interaction with your boss.

In their own words

"Everything has two handles, the one by which it may be carried, the other by which it cannot. If your brother acts unjustly, don't lay hold on the action by the handle of his injustice for by that it cannot be carried; but by the opposite, that he is your brother, that he was brought up with you; and thus you will lay hold on it, as it is to be carried."[75]

---

6. The Entitlement Challenge technique

When to use it
Use this technique when you are frustrated by other people's behavior and you feel you deserve better.

What to use it for
Use this technique to remind yourself the irrationality of feeling that you are entitled to things that you are not really entitled to.

How does the Entitlement Challenge technique work?

- In many situations, we have a feeling of entitlement. Feelings of entitlement lead to a great deal of frustration and unhappiness because in reality, in most cases, we are not entitled to anything.

- Suppose your spouse does something that you think is wrong. If you are upset with him, ask yourself this: "Maybe I am entitled to a spouse. Why do I think I am entitled to a *good* spouse?" The same applies when you are frustrated because the subway is too crowded. "I am entitled to ride the subway because I bought a ticket. Why should I think I am entitled to ride an *uncrowded* train?"

- When we challenge our feelings of entitlement often enough, we will start feeling grateful for what we have rather than be frustrated with what we don't have.

In their own words

"'But he is a bad father.'

"Well, have you any natural claim to a good father? No, only to a father.

"'My brother wrongs me.'

"Be careful then to maintain the relation you hold to him, and do not consider what he does, but what you must do if your purpose is to keep in accord with nature. For no one shall harm you, without your consent; you will only be harmed, when you think you are harmed. You will only discover what is proper to expect from a neighbor, citizen, or praetor, if you get into the habit of looking at the relations implied by each."[76]

7. The Premeditatio Malorum technique (Negative visualization)

When to use it

You can use this technique whenever you are with someone or something you love.

What to use it for

This technique helps us realize that people don't live forever, the pets you love will probably die before you do, and you may lose something beautiful in life. It is good to be constantly aware that the end of anything is unpredictable, and anything precious can be taken away from you at any time. The Premeditatio Malorum technique makes you aware that this is in the nature of things, to make you mentally accept the fact that you may lose the precious things you have in your life right now and enhance your appreciation for them.

How does the Premeditatio Malorum technique work?

Suppose you are with someone dear to you – your parents, your children, your spouse or your friend – remember that he or she is on loan to you.

1. Remember you may not see this person again. This is literally true. No one can guarantee that you will see anyone again.
2. Make sure this reminder becomes a part of your thinking.
3. Use this reminder even when you are planning something pleasant, such as going on vacation or meeting a friend.
4. Should the untoward happen in the future to your loved ones, you will be grateful for the gift that was given to you all these years and celebrate that person. To unduly grieve the loss is not a rational response because it will not bring the person back. You will only succeed in making yourself miserable for no reason.
5. Should your plans for the future be thwarted, you would not be upset, because you have already seen it in your mind's eye and are ready for it. (Psychologists call this "priming.")

Losing someone precious to you may be too intense for the application of this technique if one is not already well-prepared. The impermanence reminder technique prepares you in advance so you can apply it with greater ease when you lose someone precious.

The Premeditatio Malorum technique has an additional benefit as well. When you look at a loved one and remember that she may not live forever, that increases the appreciation of the person's presence in your life.

In their own words

"With regard to whatever objects give you delight, are useful, remind yourself of their nature... For example, if you are fond of a ceramic cup, it is only a ceramic cup ... Then if it breaks, you will not be disturbed. If you kiss your child or wife, say that you only kiss things which are human, and thus you will not be disturbed if either of them dies."[77]

---

8. The Impersonal Projection technique

When to use it

Use the Impersonal Projection technique whenever you feel that you have been wrongly treated by others or by circumstances.

What to use it for

We take everything personally. If we get cancer, we ask, "Why me?" Our favorite cup breaks. We feel it shouldn't have happened to our cup. Some thoughtless person texts while walking and bumps into us. He shouldn't have walked into us. Yet, in all such cases, there is nothing personal. The disease has nothing against you personally, the cup broke by accident, and the thoughtless person who walked into you wasn't specifically looking for you. We intuitively know this – except when it happens to us. Use this technique to remind yourself that things that happen have really nothing to do with you.

How does the Impersonal Projection technique work?

If the same things happened to other people, we wouldn't give them a second thought. Instead, we would assume that it was the natural sequence of events. If a stranger had contracted a disease, we wouldn't think, "Why her?" but rather say that it is unfortunate she got it; if a neighbor's cup broke, we would think, "It's no big deal. Accidents do happen." If we saw someone who while busily texting bumped into another person, we would probably hardly notice it. In none of these cases would we think that it has something to do with the person involved. The Impersonal Projection technique makes use of this aspect of our thinking. Here is how it works:

- Something happens that is not to your liking. For example, you catch a cold, you were short-changed in a store, or your annual medical shows that there might be some problem with your health.

- As you are about to get upset (or even after that), take a moment to calm yourself and think that it happened to a friend. You would, of course, sympathize with her, but you would also realize that it is a normal occurrence, nothing to be too upset or too worried about.

- When you project your problem to a third party, you might realize that what happened is not a terrible tragedy but what happens naturally in day-to-day life.

In their own words

"You should know that when your cup is broken, you should think as you did when your neighbor's cup was broken. Then transfer this reaction to greater things. Is another man's child or wife dead? There is no one who would not say that this is something that happens to people. But when a man's own wife or child is dead, right then he says, "Woe to me, How wretched I am!" But we should remember exactly how we feel when we hear that it has happened to others."[78]

9. The Cosmic View technique

When to use it

Use this technique whenever you get into a difficult situation that might even seem hopeless.

What to use it for

When we face a fearful situation, we see it in close-up. This exaggerates its impact. We feel that we are permanently trapped. Yet nothing lasts forever. Not even our misfortune. Everything is constantly changing. One way to get rid of that fear is to see it in a much larger context. If something seems to be an impossible situation and you feel fearful, relax and view everything with a different perspective.

How does the Cosmic View technique work?

- Sit down, relax and take a few breaths slowly and deliberately.
- Imagine that you are far above the earth and you are not even a speck.
- Then look down to see yourself on this planet and realize whatever happens to you is trivial, and you have the resources to cope with whatever happens. It will change soon anyway.

- Visualize the fourteen billion years that went before you appeared on this earth and the several billion years that will come after you are gone.

- Whatever you are facing is not as severe as it looks and surely it is within your power to adjust to whatever happens.

- Move forward in time and visualize whatever you imagine will happen has already happened. See that you have not collapsed under the weight of what happened. It is never as bad as you imagine and, even if it is, you have the resources to cope with it.

- See how things constantly change: birth into death, marriage into divorce, reputation to infamy, wealth to poverty, happiness to sadness, and often the other way round. Everything is in constant motion, and your life is just a part of this motion. There is nothing to be afraid of.

- Look back onto your life. How many things that you were afraid of five years ago do you even remember? Of those things you remember, how many came to pass?

Fear makes us worry about our reputation, losing what we have, getting what we don't want, and so on. When we view it from a cosmic perspective, we see all these things mean very little, and we can go on with our life without any of the things we are afraid of losing. We don't have to be afraid of anything. The vision will wash away the dust of fear enveloping you.

In their own words

"Gaze in wonder at the ever circling stars, as if you were floating among them; and consider the alternations of the elements, constantly changing one into another. Thinking such thoughts, you wash way the dust on earth."[79]

---

10. The Marcus' Nine technique

When to use it

This is a handy technique to use when you feel offended by the way someone speaks, acts or if someone behaves in an unacceptable way.

What to use it for

Use this technique to put things in perspective and feel free of anger, upset, and other negative feelings. Marcus' Nine is designed to restore you to a Stoic mindset of freedom and serenity.

How does Marcus' Nine technique work

Marcus' Nine is a set of 4 questions and 5 reminders proposed by Marcus Aurelius. Whenever you feel upset in any social interaction, take time out and go through these nine steps.

Marcus' Q1. Diffuse hostility.

Ask yourself: *What is my relationship to this person?* We are all made up of the same atoms or created by a creator. In either case, we are ordered by nature so we can cooperate and serve each other. This means, no matter what, we don't approach the situation with hostility towards the other person.

Marcus' Q2. Understand why he/she is upsetting you.

Ask yourself: *What compels them to behave in the way they do?* What makes them take pride in their behavior? Note that this question does not pre-judge the person, but we simply try to understand the reason for the other person's behavior.

Marcus' Q3. Evaluate the situation calmly.

Ask yourself: *Are they right?* If they are right, we should not feel unhappy about it. If they are wrong, then they are acting out of ignorance. In either case, we don't have to react immediately.

Marcus' Q4. Be compassionate.

Ask yourself: *Don't I also do similar things that are wrong?* This way you would not judge the other person harshly. Even if you think that you are perfect and consider yourself above doing anything wrong, you are a human being like others. You cannot say you are always above doing anything wrong.

Marcus' R1. Know that you cannot know the whole picture.

Remind yourself: *We cannot even know if the person is wrong because we don't know the whole context.* We don't know the other person's life and what events led up to his behaving this way.

Marcus' R2. Be aware that life's short. Don't spend it in vexation.

Remind yourself: *Our life is short.* The person who you find offensive will soon be dead. So will we. Why spend the short time we have on this earth in vexations and grievances?

Marcus' R3. Know that other people's opinions have no power to disgrace you.

Remind yourself: *If you choose not to be hurt by somebody's words or acts, you won't be hurt.* If the other person's acts are shameful, why should you spend your time brooding over it?

Marcus' R4. Know that your anger brings you pain.

Remind yourself: *What is hurting you is your anger and vexation about someone else's behavior.* By being angry, you bring pain to yourself long after the event that caused your anger is gone.

Marcus' R5. Be genuinely good. Don't fake it.

Remind yourself: *You are not genuinely being Stoic if all you do is to smile while being upset by the other people's actions.* It is important to have a genuinely pleasant disposition and not take offense at others' behavior, even if you would not act that way.

Do not try to tolerate other people's unacceptable behavior, do not flash a fake smile. Instead, realize that you are not responsible for other people's behavior; you are free and cannot be harmed by others. Once you know this, you will have fewer and fewer reasons to be upset by others.

In their own words

"Remember these nine rules, as if you have received them as a gift from the Muses and begin at last to be a man while you live."[80]

---

11. The Sun Beam Visualization technique

When to use it

Use this technique when something that is not under your control, such as your past, is preventing you from moving forward.

What to use it for

This technique is especially useful when you feel stuck and believe that you are forever blocked from moving forward.

How does the Sun Beam Visualization technique work?

- Sit down comfortably. Take a few breaths slowly and deliberately.

- Imagine the sun pouring down its light in all directions. In front of you, there is a big wall. The sunlight cannot go through the wall, and it is stopped there. It does not violently clash with the obstacle, but it does not glide or fall off either. It stays there.

- Now visualize that there is a hole in the wall. See the sunlight passing through it.

- Imagine now that the wall is completely collapsed; the sun shines immediately on the other side of what was once an obstacle.

- The sunlight reacts the same way whether the obstacle has been there for a minute or for one thousand years. The fact that the sunlight might have been obstructed by the wall for one thousand years does not stop it from going forward the moment the obstacle is removed.

- Take two or three deep breaths.

- Imagine that you are the sun and the sunbeam is your journey through life. The obstacles that stopped you from doing what you wanted to do are your past.

- Now the past is gone, so are the obstacles. Just as the sunlight is free to move forward the moment the obstacle is gone, you are free to move forward the moment the past situation has changed.

To imagine that your past – bad childhood, poverty, broken home – is still with you is like the sunlight believing that it cannot go forward because it was obstructed so long. Contemplate living like the sun whose light moves forward the moment the obstacle is removed – your past does not have power over you unless you believe it does.

In their own words

"To understand the property of a sunbeam, watch the light as it streams through a darkened room through a narrow chink... not clashing violently or furiously against the obstacle it encounters, nor yet falling away in despair."[81]

---

12. The South Indian Monkey Trap
Visualization technique

When we imagine that we are trapped by the past – be it a dysfunctional family, impoverished childhood, or having had to face traumatic incidents – if we don't let go of the past, it may affect our future.

When to use it

Use this technique whenever you feel that the past has such a strong hold on you that there is no way you can break free of it.

What to use it for

The technique is a powerful way of visualizing that the freedom we seek is right here, and the steel trap of the past is a figment of our imagination. The visualization is about how monkeys are being caught in South India because they can't let go even when their life is at stake.

How does the South Indian Monkey Trap Visualization technique work?

- Imagine a monkey trap, which is attached to a stake that consists of a hollowed-out coconut with some rice inside.

- There is a hole large enough for the monkey to get its hand in but once it grabs the rice inside its fist gets too large to come out. The villagers are coming to get the monkey.

- All that monkey needs to do is to open its fist, and it is free. Yet it won't. It doesn't realize that what is restraining it is not the trap itself, but its failure to see that it can simply free itself by releasing what is in its hand. It's trapped.

- Now imagine yourself to be a monkey that is caught in the trap. The rice that you are holding onto is your past.

- Now you have a choice. You can hold on to your past like the monkey holding on to its rice, unwilling to let go. The result would be the same for you as it would be for the monkey: loss of freedom.

- Just as the monkey can simply release the rice and go free, you can let go of the past and go free. It's as simple as that. Let go of the past.

Always remember what is under your control and what is not. Do not try to control what is not under your control. The past is not under your control. It is not controlling you either unless you believe it is. What you can do now is under your control. Let go of the past.

In their own words

"[E]ven if all this is true, it is over and gone. What benefit is there in reviewing past sufferings, and in being unhappy, just because once you were unhappy?"[82]

PART V

REFERENCE SECTION

A Reading Plan and Notes

A Reading Plan

If you would like to pursue the ideas presented in this book, I recommend that you start with a general introduction to philosophies of the good life. For a lively introduction, I suggest that you get a copy of the book by Jules Evans *Philosophy for Life and Other Dangerous Situations*, published by New World Library.

If you want to start with a simple reading plan for Stoicism, here is what I would suggest:

Level 1: Basic

1. Epictetus. *The Good Life Handbook*, published by The Stoic Gym (A 2016 rendering of Epictetus' *Enchiridion*, rendered in contemporary style). Electronic edition available free at Amazon, and other online retailers. OR

The Art of Living (Epictetus' *Enchiridion* expressed in contemporary English by Sharon LeBell, published by Harper SanFrancisco, 2007. Clear and easy to follow.)

2. Seneca. *Letters from a Stoic* (Translated by Richard Mortt Gummere and published by Enhanced Media. Just $0.99 for the Kindle edition. An excellent introduction to Seneca.)

3. Aurelius, Marcus. *Meditations*. (Translated by Maxwell Staniforth and published by Penguin, 2004) OR

Meditations by Gregory Hays. (Hays' lucid translation was published by The Modern Library in 2002. However, be warned, it can be cryptic at times. I prefer to read Hays' book along with Staniforth's to make sure I understand what Hays means at times.)

If you buy these books on Kindle, the set of three books would cost you less than $25 (as of late 2016). This should also provide you with a clear understanding of what Stoicism is and how you can apply it to your own life.

Level 2: Intermediate

At this stage, you have two choices 2a or 2b. Choose 2a if you need to understand in greater depth what you learned in Level 1. Choose Level 2b if you are more interested in an in-depth interpretation of ancient philosophers, especially Marcus Aurelius. Choose both if you are keen on learning much more about Stoicism.

Level 2a

1. Epictetus. *Of Human Freedom.* (This is extracted from Robert Dobbin's *Discourses and Selected Writings* (2008), both published by Penguin.)

I recommend *Discourses* but, if you are short of time, *Of Human Freedom* would do just fine. Even Dobbin's *Discourses and Selected Writings* does not contain the complete version of *Discourses.* For a complete version, I recommend *The Discourses of Epictetus* (which also includes The Handbook, and Fragments), translated by Robin Hard and published by Everyman, 1995.

2. Seneca. *Dialogues, The Complete Collection.* (Again, published by Enhanced Media, and the Kindle edition is very inexpensive at $1.)

3. Rufus, Musonius. *Lectures and Fragments.* (You can get the Kindle edition just for $1.)

Level 2b

1. Hadot, Pierre. *The Inner Citadel.* (An excellent interpretation of Marcus Aurelius' *Meditations*, published by Harvard University Press, 2001.)

2. Hadot, Pierre. *Philosophy as a Way of Life.* Wiley-Blackwell, 1995 (The purpose of this book is to show how you can use philosophy to live better.)

Level 3: On your own

At this level, there are too many contenders. I encourage you to explore what is available on your own. And if you have gone through the first two levels, you don't need my recommendation anyway. Some available books may appeal to you more, some less. You may want to browse the books first before buying.

Some people may prefer to start with one of the following books below rather than the ones I recommend in Level 1 or 2. This is personal preference. I prefer to read what the philosophers actually said before reading interpretations of what they said. So my recommendations follow my preference: starting with the original, *then* reading the interpretation.

In no particular order (except alphabetical), here are some recent books on Stoicism.

- Forstater, Mark (2000) *The Spiritual Teachings of Marcus Aurelius*. Harper Collins. (Yes, this is the same Mark Forstater who produced the film *Monty Python and the Holy Grail*.)

- Holiday, Ryan (2016) *Ego is the Enemy*. Portfolio.

- Holiday, Ryan (2014) *The Obstacle is the Way*. Portfolio.

- Irvine, William (2008) *A Guide to the Good Life*. Oxford University Press.

- Morris, Tom (2004) *The Stoic Art of Living*. Open Court, 2004.

- Robertson, Donald (2013) *Stoicism and the Art of Happiness*. Teach Yourself Series.

- Robertson, Donald (2012) *Build Your Resilience*. Teach Yourself Series.

- Ussher, Patrick (2014, 2016) *Stoicism Today, Selected Writings* (Volume 1 and Volume 2). CreateSpace Independent Publishing Platform.

Notes

[1] Epictetus. *Discourses*. Book II.19.29.

[2] Thoreau, Henry David. *Walden; or, Life in the Woods*. (First published in 1854. Several editions are still in print.)

[3] Epictetus. *Discourses*. Book II.19.29

[4] If this is not already obvious, this book is not a scholarly work on Stoicism. While I tried to be as true to Stoic principles as I can, because many good translations of Stoic works are not in contemporary English, I freely adapted them to correspond to modern usage while trying to be careful not to change their meaning. If you are interested in getting the precise quote even of passages where I have used quotation marks, please refer to one of the traditional translations. This should be an easy task since I provide the references and many Stoic books are (literally) freely available online.

[5] Epictetus, *Discourses*, Book I.17.28.

[6] Epictetus. *Discourses*. Book I.1.28-30 (My exposition here is based on Robert Dobbin's translation published by Penguin in 2008.)

[7] Epictetus. *The Golden Sayings of Epictetus*. XXII (Based on the translation and arrangement by Hastings Crossley.)

[8] You can read a first-hand account of Dr. Cornum's ordeal in her book (with *Peter Copeland*) *She Went to War: The Rhonda Cornum Story*. I first read about Rhonda Cornum in *Philosophy for Life and Other Dangerous Situations* by Jules Evans, London: Rider Books 2012.

[9] *Time*, Friday, March 28, 2003.

[10] Frankl, Victor (1959) *Man's Search for Meaning*, London: Random House.

[11] Aurelius, Marcus. *Meditations.* Book VII.67.

[12] *Thoughts of Marcus Aurelius.* Long's translation edited by Edwin Ginn. The quote appears in the section "The Philosophy of Marcus Aurelius."

[13] Tacitus 15. (Referenced by Irvine, William B. *A Guide to the Good Life.* OUP 2008.

[14] The Stoic Gym has published a new rendering of *Enchiridion* under the title *The Good Life Handbook*. The online version of the book is available for free on Amazon and other major online bookstores.

[15] http://news.bbc.co.uk/2/hi/health/4381924.stm (Retrieved September 6, 2016).

[16] Wolfe, Tom (2001) *A Man in Full.* Dial Press, Reprint edition.

[17] Wade, Morgan (2011) *The Last Stoic.* Hidden Brook Press.

[18] Seneca, L.A. *Moral Essays.* (Translated by J.W. Basore), II.425.

[19] Epictetus. *Discourses.* Book I.1.32 .

[20] Lipsenthal, Lee (2011) *Enjoy Every Sandwich.* Random House.

[21] Epictetus. *Enchiridion.* 5.

[22] Lipsenthal, Lee (2011) *Enjoy Every Sandwich.* Random House, 2011.

[23] Epictetus. *Discourses,* Book IV4.39.

[24] Aurelius, Marcus. *Meditations.* Book IV.7.

[25] Aurelius, Marcus. *Meditations.* Book XII.1.

[26] Seneca, L.A. Letters From a Stoic. LXXXIII.

[27] Epictetus. *Discourses.* Book III.20.4. Translator: Robert Dobbin (2008). Penguin.

[28] Schoch, Robert (2006) *The Secrets of Happiness*. London:Scribner.

[29] Aurelius, Marcus. *Meditations*. Book XII.1.

[30] Epictetus. *Discourses*, Book III.9.22.

[31] Pirsig, Robert M. (2006) *Zen and the Art of Motorcycle Maintenance*. HarperTorch, 1st edition.

[32] Aurelius, Marcus. *Meditations*. VIII.57

[33] Epictetus. *Discourses*, Book III.9.22.

[34] Epictetus. *Discourses*, Book III.13.11.

[35] Epictetus. *Discourses*, Book IV.4.25. (Robert Dobbin's translation)

[36] Epictetus. *Discourses*, Book III.16.16.

[37] Epictetus. *Discourses*, Book IV.1.109.

[38] Epictetus. *Discourses*, Book IV.4.34.

[39] Marcus Aurelius *Meditations*. Book IV.7.

[40] Epictetus. *Enchiridion*, 43.

[41] Aurelius, Marcus. *Meditations*. Book IX.18.

[42] Seneca. *Letters From a Stoic: Epistulae Morales ad Lucilium*.

[43] Shakespeare, William. *Julius Caesar*.

44 Epictetus. *Discourses*, Book I.2.19-21.

[45] Khayyam, Omar (1889) *The Rubaiyat of Omar Khayyam*. Translated by Edward Fitzgerald, Fifth Edition.

[46] Shirer, William (1979) *Gandhi: A Memoir*. Simon and Schuster.

[47] Sorabji, Richard (2012) *Gandhi and the Stoics*. University Of Chicago Press; First Edition.

48 Aurelius, Marcus. *Meditations*. Book V.20.

[49] Aurelius, Marcus. *Meditations*. Book VI.6.

[50] Epictetus. *Discourses,* Book IV.1.29.

[51] Epictetus. *Discourses,* Book IV.1.29.

[52] Aurelius, Marcus. *Meditations,* VII.48.

[53] Epictetus. *Enchiridion,* 30.

[54] Aurelius, Marcus. *Meditations.* Book VII.8.

[55] Leahy, Robert (2006) *Worry Cure.* Harmony, 1 edition.

[56] Seneca. *Dialogues.* (Translated by Aubrey Stewart and Damian Stevenson, 2015), Chapter IX.

[57] Epictetus. *Discourses,* Book IV.1.103. Translator: Robert Dobbin (2008). Penguin.

[58] I first read a synopsis of this story in Timothy Miller's wonderful book *How to Want What You Have.* Henry Holt & Co. 1994. (Unfortunately, this book is out-of-print now.)

[59] "Strange Wine" in Harlan Ellison's *Amazing Stories,* NY: Harper & Row, 1976.

[60] Seneca, L.A. *Moral Essays.* (Translated by J.W. Basore), I.161.

[61] Seneca., L.A. *Moral Essays.* (Translated by J.W. Basore), II.283.

[62] Seneca, L.A. *Moral Essays.* (Translated by J.W. Basore)

[63] Aurelius, Marcus. *Meditations,* XII.3,4. (Hadot, Pierre. *The Inner Citadel.* Harvard University Press, 2001.)

[64] Carlos Castenada (1975) *Journey to Ixtalen.* Simon & Schuster.

[65] *The Morals of Seneca: A Selection of his Prose, based on the translation* by Sir Roger L'Estrange, edited by Walter Clode; London: Walter Scott, Ltd., 1888; pp. 3-5

[66] Epictetus. *Discourses and Selected Writings.* Discourses, Book II.18. 13-14. Translator: Robert Dobbin (2008). Penguin.

[67] Seneca L.A. *Letters From a Stoic: Epistulae Morales ad Lucilium.* (Translated by Richard Mott Gummere). Enhanced Media.

[68] *The Morals of Seneca: A Selection of his Prose, based on the translation* by Sir Roger L'Estrange, edited by Walter Clode; London: Walter Scott, Ltd., 1888; pp. 3-5.

[69] Laertius, Diogenes. *Lives and Opinions of Eminent Philosophers.*

[70] Aurelius, Marcus, *Meditations*, Book II.1.

[71] Aurelius, Marcus, *Meditations*, Book V.1.

[72] *The Morals of Seneca: A Selection of his Prose, based on the translation* by Sir Roger L'Estrange, edited by Walter Clode; London: Walter Scott, Ltd., 1888.

[73] Epictetus, *Discourses* II.18.12.13.

[74] Epictetus, *Enchiridion*, 1.

[75] Epictetus, *Enchiridion* 43.

[76] Epictetus. *Discourses*, Book III.10.19.

[77] Epictetus, *Enchiridion*, 3.

[78] Epictetus, *Enchiridion*, 26.

[79] Aurelius, Marcus *Meditations*, Book VII.47.

[80] Aurelius, Marcus *Meditations*, Book XI.18.

[81] Aurelius, Marcus *Meditations*, Book VIII.5.7

[82] Seneca L.A. *Letters from a Stoic.* LXXIII, Richard Mottt Gummere's translation.

The epigraph is from *The Golden Sayings of Epictetus.* XXIX.

And don't forget your free copy of the book,

A Fortunate Storm
A Companion Volume *to Unshakable Freedom*

Unshakable Freedom is based on Stoic teachings.

But how did Stoicism come about?

Three unconnected events – a shipwreck in Piraeus, a play in Thebes, and the banishment of a rebel in Turkey – connected three unrelated individuals to give birth to a philosophy. It was to endure two thousand years and offer hope and comfort to hundreds of thousands of people along the way.

The Fortunate Storm is the story of how Stoicism came about. You can get a FREE COPY of the entire book at the link below:

http://www.TheStoicGym.com/fortunatestormfree

ABOUT THE AUTHOR

Dr. Chuck Chakrapani is President of Leger Analytics and Distinguished Visiting Professor at Ryerson University. He has been a long-term, but embarrassingly inconsistent, practitioner of Stoicism. His personal website is ChuckChakrapani.com. For additional free materials on Stoicism, please log in to TheStoicGym.com